ROME AND THE BARBARIANS

A BODLEY HEAD ARCHAEOLOGY

Rome and the Barbarians

BARRY CUNLIFFE

Drawings by
SHIRLEY FELTS
Maps and diagrams by
EDGAR HOLLOWAY

THE BODLEY HEAD · London Sydney Toronto

THE BODLEY HEAD ARCHAEOLOGIES
Edited by MAGNUS MAGNUSSON

MAGNUS MAGNUSSON *Introducing Archaeology*
                            Viking Expansion Westwards
T. G. H. JAMES *The Archaeology of Ancient Egypt*
RONALD HARKER *Digging Up the Bible Lands*
REYNOLD HIGGINS *The Archaeology of Minoan Crete*
JOHN HAY *Ancient China*
PAUL JOHNSTONE *The Archaeology of Ships*

IN PREPARATION

DAVID BROWN *The Archaeology of Anglo-Saxon England*
PETER HARBISON *The Archaeology of Ireland*
ANNA RITCHIE *The Archaeology of Early Scotland*
KENNETH HUDSON *The Archaeology of Industry*

FRONTISPIECE
This relief on a
distance-slab from
Bridgeness on the
Antonine Wall in
Scotland dates from
the mid-second
century AD and shows
defeated Britons being
trampled by a Roman
cavalry man.

© Barry Cunliffe 1975
Drawings and maps © The Bodley Head 1975
ISBN 0 370 01578 9
Printed in Great Britain for
The Bodley Head Ltd
9 Bow Street, London WC2E 7AL
by BAS Printers Limited, Wallop, Hampshire
First published 1975

CONTENTS

ACKNOWLEDGMENTS

Thanks are due to the following for permission to reproduce black-and-white photographs: National Museum of Antiquities of Scotland, frontispiece; Roger-Viollet, Paris, pages 23, 30 and 32; Photographie Giraudon, Paris, page 29; Institute of Archaeology, Oxford, pages 41, 42 and 47; Department of Aerial Photography, Cambridge, pages 49, 50 and 117; Fototeca Unione, Rome, page 55; the Mansell Collection, London, pages 57, 62, 66 and 70; Kunsthistorische Museums, Vienna, page 88; National Museum of Denmark, Copenhagen, page 90; the Rijksmuseum van Oudheden te Leiden, pages 93 and 94; Michael Rouillard, pages 101, 107 and 108; A. W. Rule, page 115.

Thanks are due for permission to reproduce coloured material: Diafrance, Paris, facing pages 48 and 49; National Museum of Antiquities, Bucharest, facing page 64; Institute of Archaeology, Oxford, facing pages 65, 80 and 81; David Leigh, facing page 96; British Tourist Authority, facing page 97; the Trustees of the British Museum, jacket. The drawings on pages 11 and 14 and the map on page 13 are based on *The Sunday Times* wall-chart 'The Roman Army'; the map on page 27 is from *Roman Gaul* by O. Brogan (Bell, 1953); the map on page 37 is from *De Vita Agricolae* by R. Ogilvy and Sir I. Richmond (Oxford University Press, 1967); the drawing on page 44 is based on Sir Ian Richmond's reconstruction at the Institute of Archaeology, Oxford; the map on page 58 is based on one from *A Short History of the Roman Empire* by Wells and Barrow (Methuen); the drawings on pages 63 and 77 are based on photographs in the collection of the Institute of Archaeology, Oxford; the map on page 87 is based, with additions, on one from *Rome Beyond the Imperial Frontiers* by Sir Mortimer Wheeler (Bell, 1954); the diagrams on pages 111 and 113 are based on similar ones in Dr Mertens' excavation report on Oudenburg.

INTRODUCTION

This book was conceived in eastern Belgium, it was thought about in Hungary and Czechoslovakia, it took shape in Holland and Tunisia and it was written in England. These countries have one thing in common: they were once wholly or partly within the Roman Empire. Visit a museum in any one of them and you will be bound to find mass-produced Roman pottery or coins which would have been as familiar to a native from the northern fringe of the Sahara as to one from the forests of Moravia.

The Roman world fascinates people. It is partly its sheer scale and monumentality, partly that Roman history is full of marvellous stories, but it must also be that through Roman archaeology it is possible to get very close to the people themselves and their everyday lives. This is why so many full-time and part-time archaeologists have come to the broader aspects of the subject through a childhood interest in the Romans. The Romans have enthralled generations: they will continue to do so.

This book is an attempt to select a number of sites and events which show in strong relief the relationships between Romans and barbarians and the ways in which archaeologists go about discovering them. The choice is, of course, a personal one, but if it has any merit, it is that it reflects, fairly, something of the range of the subject.

In writing the book I have constantly been reminded of how much the subject in general, and I in particular, owe to the encouragement of Ian Richmond. His great scholarship and personal kindness, both so willingly given, will remain a fond memory. I would also like to record my thanks to Professor Sheppard Frere for reading the manuscript of this book and offering many wise suggestions, and to all the archaeologists in the countries I have visited, who have given me so much of their valuable time.

1

Rome on the Eve of the Empire

In the eighth century BC, Rome was little more than a group of peasant communities occupying simple timber huts—by AD 14 it was a magnificent city, reigning supreme over an empire stretching from Spain to Syria and from the Rhine to the Sahara. That period of eight hundred years which led to the emergence of Rome as a ruthless imperial power has had its effects on world history ever since.

The rise of Rome was not a gentle progression, nor was it characterised by a consistent nobility of purpose. Greed and personal gain often intermingled with mob violence and officially-condoned reigns of terror, but behind the moments of horror lay the stolid strength of the average Roman, brought up in three traditional virtues, serious-mindedness, piety and simplicity. It was this mixture that was to make Rome great. The Greek historian, Polybius, who was present at the Roman destruction of Carthage in 146 BC, believed that the greatness of Rome was to be explained by its perfect political constitution in which monarchy, democracy and aristocracy were carefully blended and balanced, no one element being dominant. He was saying much the same thing—Romans and the Roman state had within themselves all the elements that made for greatness.

From the time that the city of Rome emerged from the domination of the powerful Etruscan state to the north, in the early part of the fifth century BC, until the beginning of the wars with Carthage in the third century BC, much of the energy of the developing state was absorbed in fighting and diplomacy on the Italian mainland, both with the indigenous population and with the hordes of Celtic invaders who poured across the Alps and spread south into the peninsula in or after 390 BC. Yet by the end of this formative phase, the city-state of Rome had risen to a pre-eminent position as the centre of a great confederacy of Italian tribes and cities. So great was the power of Rome that it now began to come into conflict with the other Mediterranean powers, the Hellenistic kingdoms to the east and Carthage to the west.

The wars with Carthage were the inevitable result of the two states physically confronting each other, first in Sicily and later in Spain. The final, and for Carthage, fatal, confrontation, came when Rome, still not satisfied that it had brought its enemy to heel, and encouraged by those Romans whose capitalist interests were adversely affected by the power of the Carthaginians' trading empire, took the final decision to wipe out the city once and for all. It is said that one of the rich Roman landowners, Cato, on returning from Carthage, held up a luxurious bunch of Carthaginian figs in the Roman Senate to strengthen his point that the wealth and productivity of Carthage was a threat to the Roman state and to the trading interests of the land-holding aristocracy. In 146 BC, after three years of war, Carthage was obliterated and most of her inhabitants slaughtered. Polybius tells how Scipio Aemilianus, the Roman general who destroyed the city, looked at what he had done and

The Roman provinces in 100 BC.

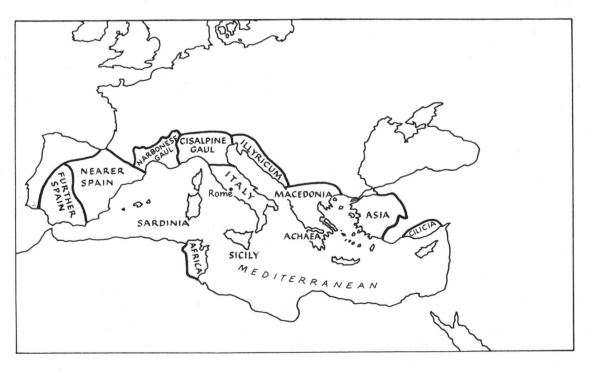

wept for the fate of his enemy. 'This is a glorious moment,' he said, 'and yet I am seized with fear and foreboding that some day the same end will befall my own country.'

Rome's concerns with the East, with Macedonia, Greece, Asia Minor and Syria, were more tangled, but once drawn into the petty squabbles of the Hellenistic rulers, it was difficult for the government to opt out, and the East was to remain a fertile theatre for many a would-be power-hunter in which to stir up trouble. However, after the annexation of Macedonia, Rome's first long involvement was neatly concluded with the defeat of the Greek Achaean League in 146 BC and the destruction of the rich commercial city of Corinth.

In a single year, 146 BC, Rome's two greatest commercial rivals, Carthage and Corinth, had been wiped out and firm footholds had been obtained in both the East Mediterranean and North Africa. Not long afterwards, the defeat of the fierce Celtiberians in northern Spain in 133 BC greatly extended Rome's hold on the Iberian Peninsula, while in the same year King Attalus III bequeathed to Rome his kingdom of Pergamon, which thereafter became the province of Asia. A few years later Roman armies annexed much of the prosperous territory of southern France. Thus in the second half of the second century BC, Rome's territories had spread to all parts of the civilised world: the foundations of the Empire were now well and truly laid.

A Roman legionary.

With expansion outward came social change at home. The old values declined, and there arose a strong feeling that the power of the aristocratic Senate should be curtailed. The new democrats were led by two brothers, Tiberius and Gaius Gracchus, both of whom met violent deaths at the hands of their opponents. Their activities, however well intentioned, led to little more than a violent and prolonged period of social conflict and civil war which was to last for about a century. During this time many famous people rose and fell; Marius the army reformer, Sulla his enemy and restorer of the old order, and towards the end, Caesar, Pompey and Augustus. All these men, ambitious for power, saw the army as an essential support to their personal aspirations. For Marius and Sulla the army was simply a means of strength: for Caesar and Pompey, on the other hand, it was also a means of gaining military prestige by conquest. The two men were rivals, and when by 62 BC Pompey returned triumphant to Rome, having created two new provinces in the East, Syria and Bithynia with Pontus, it was only natural that Caesar should look for an equivalent chance of military conquest

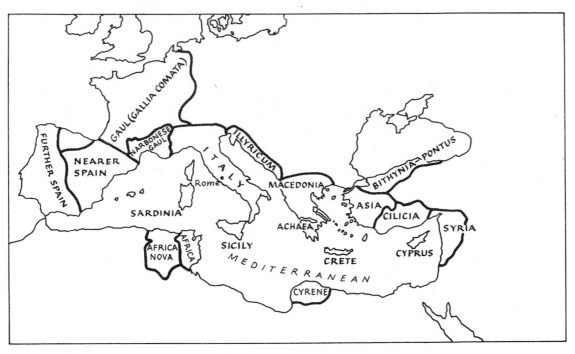

The provinces in 44 BC after Caesar's conquests.

in the West. Three years later he was to begin his famous conquest of Gaul.

The first century BC was a time of change both at home and abroad—a time when the Roman state was rapidly evolving, usually under pressure or compulsion from ambitious leaders eager for the support of the masses. It was also a time when the military machine was brought to a fine pitch of readiness: it was a fierce, destructive period. When the blood had finally congealed after the great battles which culminated in the deaths of Antony and Cleopatra, only one man was left in power—Octavius, soon to be recognised as the first Emperor, Augustus.

It was Augustus who, from 27 BC until his death in AD 14, created the basis of the Empire. He restored the capital and rebuilt its temples, he gently moulded government into an acceptable and efficient administration, and he constructed a unified professional army. In short, he was both an innovator and a consolidator. He fully realised that, with a growing empire, Rome needed a thoroughly disciplined standing army. The heart of his force were the legions, each composed of between five and six thousand Roman citizens divided into centuries of eighty men under the command of a centurion. Although in Caesar's time all kinds of provincials were recruited to the legions, Augustus reverted to the strict policy that only citizens were eligible, which meant inhabitants of Italy and a smaller group of citizens living in the larger provincial towns. From now on the legions were never stationed in Italy but along the provincial frontiers and in other likely trouble spots. His second reform was the introduction of regular units of auxiliary troops drawn from among the provincials or contributed by allies. These were arranged in regiments called *alae* and *cohortes*, cavalry and infantry, and were attached to the legions to carry out specialised functions and to lighten the burden of the legionaries. Quite often the auxiliary detachments were fighters highly skilled in a particular type of warfare like Syrian archers, Balearic slingers or Thracian cavalry spearmen. Augustus also introduced a standing navy divided into two squadrons, one based at Misenum in southern Italy, the other at Ravenna on the Adriatic, but the navy was regarded as very second-rate compared with the army—practically anyone could join.

Perhaps the most significant of the Augustan reforms was that military matters were no longer in the hands of the Senate, the popular assembly, or the annually elected magistrates—they were

The Empire at its maximum extent *c.* AD 200.

solely the prerogative of the Emperor. Augustus had thus assured the continuation of power for himself and for his successors.

During the phase of maximum expansion, roughly 150 BC to AD 150, Rome came into contact with civilised peoples like the Greeks, the Carthaginians and the eastern Hellenistic states, as well as more primitive peoples—the barbarians. 'Barbarian' comes from a Greek word which literally means the people who say 'ba ba', or in other words speak unintelligible languages. In the following chapters we will examine some of these confrontations: Caesar against the Gauls, Agricola against the tribes of Scotland and Trajan against the Dacians. Each conflict posed different problems; each had different results, but together they give a vivid impression of what it must have been like to have been a Roman soldier or a barbarian fighting for different worlds and values in some distant part of Europe.

But the story of Rome and the barbarians is more than one of conflict: once an area had been subdued it had to be governed, which meant implanting the trappings of Roman administration while at the same time allowing native customs and beliefs to survive. This delicate process of integration is particularly well displayed by the work of Hungarian archaeologists on towns and settlements in what was the Roman province of Pannonia (Chapter 5). To see something of the survival of native spirit, however, we must consider a selection of the gods and goddesses from north-west Europe (Chapter 6).

The Roman Empire collapsed in a far shorter time than it had taken for it to develop. Ineffectual, fragmented government within, confronted a vigorous and increasingly mobile population without. The frontiers buckled, towns were overrun, and the population was thrown back increasingly on its own resources. In Chapter 7 we examine some of these forces at work and see how in a few decades following AD 400 the Roman Empire vanished.

A Roman centurion.

2

An Emperor in Caesar's Footsteps

By the year 59 BC the Roman province in southern France was secure and some parts of it were well on the way towards assimilating a Roman life style, but beyond to the north lay *Gallia Comata* or 'long-haired Gaul', where lived a quarrelsome people constantly squabbling among themselves, a society in whose extreme form of rigorous class structure lay the seeds of its own destruction. According to Caesar there were only two classes of any significance, the warrior leaders and the Druids; the rest were subservient peasants little better than slaves. All this was of little concern to the Roman administration; a divided people was unlikely to pose a threat to security, and anyway the local *oppida* (native capitals) provided lucrative markets for the Roman merchants and traders to exploit. But suddenly a sinister new threat appeared—in the north-east, German war bands from across the Rhine decided to intervene.

Ariovistus, king of a German tribe called the Suebi, was incited to take sides in a quarrel between two Gallic tribes in *Gallia Comata*, the Aedui and the Sequani. The Sequani agreed to give him land in Alsace in return for his military support; but as soon as the deal had been made, Ariovistus and his supporters demanded more territory to consolidate and extend their foothold across the Rhine. Too late the Gauls realised that the floodgates to German invasion were open. The Aedui took the only course open to them—they appealed for help to their traditional allies, Rome. At precisely the same moment the Helvetii, who occupied the territory that is now western Switzerland, decided to migrate west into Gaul, partly because the population had outgrown the size of the available land, and partly because of the new German threat from beyond the

Rhine, and now from Alsace. Such a migration could seriously affect the balance of power in the west.

To the ambitious forty-two-year-old consul, Julius Caesar, this must have seemed a heaven-sent opportunity, a chance for great military victories and for vast territorial conquest. Few men could have resisted the temptation. He realised, he said, that Gaul was destined either to become German or to become Roman. In eight years of brilliant campaigning, he was to make sure that Rome triumphed.

Until quite recently the exploits of Julius Caesar have been common knowledge to educated generations steeped in the Latin of Caesar's own account of those campaigns, the famous *Gallic Wars*. It is probably true to say that in the latter part of the nineteenth century the *Gallic Wars* was among the most widely read books in the western world. Full of military glory and telling the simple story of the triumph of organised imperialism over unruly and half-civilised natives, Caesar's war commentaries were in close sympathy with the beliefs and aspirations of the time. It is little wonder that when Louis Napoleon, the nephew of Napoleon I, came to power in France in 1852 as Napoleon III, head of the French Second Empire, he developed a keen interest in Caesar's Gallic exploits.

Napoleon III had done much to re-establish the prestige of France both in the minds of its people and abroad. The economy was stable in spite of the depressions and worldwide crises of the mid-1850s, and his court was brilliant and lively—particularly after his marriage to a beautiful Spanish countess in 1853. Internally France prospered: stability and national pride were given free expression in a series of elaborate fêtes and military reviews, and in 1855 the great Paris Exhibition was staged to demonstrate to the world that France was once more a foremost power (and incidentally to counter-balance the impact of the London Exhibition held in 1851). The new Emperor was fascinated by archaeology. In 1862 he founded the Museum of National Antiquities at Saint-Germain-en-Laye, to serve as a focus for his growing interest in the past of his country. On more than one occasion politicians who preach nationalism have turned to archaeology for support. For Napoleon III the central figure was, of course, Julius Caesar, and in 1865 he was to publish his two famous volumes entitled *Histoire de Jules César*.

Caesar was an immensely popular subject for Napoleon and his entourage, and not surprisingly the Emperor became equated in the

OPPOSITE
Plan of Alesia,
showing the lines
of the Roman siege
works, from Napoleon
III's famous *Histoire
de Jules César*.

minds of many, and even perhaps himself, with his Roman pre-
decessor. Those opposed to the Napoleonic regime championed
Caesar's celebrated Gallic opponent, the gallant Vercingetorix, who
thenceforth became the symbol of the oppressed Gallic spirit in its
constant fight against greater external odds. For many Frenchmen,
even today, the valour of the Gauls and the defeats they suffered at
the hands of Julius Caesar are seen to characterise a recurring
tragic theme running through French history. The enormous popu-
larity of the comic strip character, Asterix, is in part a reflection of
the modern generation laughing at the half-understood attitudes of
the recent past.

A central concern of Napoleon III in his pursuit of Caesar was to
try to establish the actual ground over which the general had fought
his campaigns and to define the positions of the camps and siege-
works of the Roman army. To achieve this he created a special
archaeological corps under the command of the Alsatian-born
Colonel Stoffel. At one time Stoffel's force numbered as many as
three hundred, and included for a short while, as one of its in-
spectors, Prosper Mérimée, the writer responsible for what was
later to become the libretto of the opera *Carmen*! For five years, from
1860 to 1865, Stoffel and his corps of diggers laboured, from the
migration route of the Helvetii to the battlefield of Alesia, faithfully
tracing Caesar's military works. Although mistakes were inevitably
made, Stoffel was a highly competent field archaeologist and must
be classed as one of the pioneers in the application of dirt archaeology to historical problems.

When, in 1899, Theodore Rice Holmes was completing his great
book *Caesar's Conquest of Gaul* (still the standard work on the
subject) he wrote to the ageing Colonel Stoffel and asked him to
explain something of his archaeological methods. The old man
replied at length, describing in basic terms how a disturbance such as
a silted-up ditch could be recognised when seen in section. He then
went on to explain that, having defined a location where he sus-
pected one of Caesar's camps to be, he set his workmen to dig
parallel trial trenches two feet (0·61 metres) wide and sixty to ninety
feet (twenty to thirty metres) apart, stripping off the topsoil down
to the undisturbed subsoil. As soon as a disturbance was en-
countered, he enlarged the trench to six feet (1·83 metres) wide in
order to make sure that it was a ditch and to ascertain its direction.
Then he would cut five or six trenches along the line of each side of
the camp to define its position precisely. At Gergovia, near Cler-

mont-Ferrand, Stoffel traced two Caesarian camps, the outlines of both of which he defined with markers. When a new campaign of excavation was carried out just before the Second World War, the archaeologists found Stoffel's markers to be dead accurate every time. Sometimes the work was on a limited scale, but at Alesia his research took more than two years to complete because, as he explained, they had to determine not only the position of the camps but also miles of siege-works: more than three hundred workers were employed! Although there is nothing particularly original in the Colonel's approach, for the 1860s, it is the sheer organised good sense of this massively conceived project that now impresses. Rice Holmes' rather damning comment on the old man's letter— 'Substantially, he confirmed my own preconceived notions, and his method was identical with that which is followed by Professor Haverfield and other well-known investigators'—does less than justice to this pioneer of field archaeology.

Before discussing some of the results produced by archaeologists who have attempted to study the remains of Caesar's campaigns, we must look very briefly at what happened in those eight eventful years of his consulship.

Faced with the twin threat of Ariovistus of the Suebi and of the migrating Helvetii, Caesar acted promptly. The immediate problem was to stop the Helvetii: to this end he marched to Geneva to prevent the tribe from crossing the Rhône. Thus far he was successful, but the natives felt no less compelled to move on, and in order to avoid the Romans they turned north through the territory of the Sequani. It was essentially a peaceful act of non-confrontation, but Caesar pursued them and in a single short campaign, during which almost half the native force was slaughtered, they were defeated and forced to return to their homeland. With their depleted numbers the problem of overpopulation was no longer so acute, and the Romans could feel safe again now that the territory of western Switzerland was once more populated by non-Germans. After brief discussions with the leaders of the Aedui at their *oppidum* of Bibracte, Caesar now moved against Ariovistus. The king was soundly defeated and the Roman army set up its winter quarters near Besançon in the territory of the Sequani. It was the autumn of 58 BC, and Gaul lay unconquered and waiting.

It was clear that Caesar's next target would be the territory of the Belgic tribes who lived between the Seine and the Rhine. The subjugation of this region was essential to the security of the rest of

Gaul, since it was across this area that any German attack would have to come. During the winter months the Belgae prepared for war, but while some of the tribes wished to stand against the Romans, others saw their salvation in an alliance. At the beginning of the campaigning season of 57 BC, Caesar was met by envoys from the Remi, with whom he concluded a treaty of friendship before marching on to destroy the massed Belgic force in the land of the Bellovaci around Beauvais. Resistance was now fragmented, but it required a series of mopping-up operations before the Belgae could be regarded as finally subdued. The slaughter was considerable: one tribe, the Nervii, was almost totally annihilated. In Caesar's own words, he had brought 'the name and nation of the Nervii almost to utter destruction'. While all this was under way, one of Caesar's subordinates, Publius Crassus, supported by a single legion, was in the west receiving the formal submission of 'the maritime states which border upon the ocean'—in other words, the tribes of western Normandy and Brittany. By the autumn of 57 the encirclement of Gaul was complete, and while Crassus wintered near the Loire, Caesar could return in triumph to Rome to claim that 'all of Gaul is in peace'.

His assessment soon proved to be inaccurate. It seems that rumours had spread that Caesar was planning to invade Britain the following year, and the maritime tribes (particularly those of the Breton peninsula, who controlled much of the Channel trade) objected. Rebellion flared, led by the seafaring Veneti of Brittany. Caesar's response was immediate and decisive: his second-in-command, Labienus, was sent with a cavalry detachment to demonstrate a Roman presence among the Belgae, Crassus was sent to Aquitania in western France to prevent reinforcements being sent up the west coast, while three legions commanded by Sabinus were dispatched to northern Brittany and Normandy to attack the rebels on land. Meanwhile in the Loire estuary, a Roman fleet was constructed to deal with the Venetic navy. With these brilliantly planned preparations now complete, Caesar himself marched on the Veneti. The two great fleets met off the south Breton coast near Quiberon. The battle was hard fought, but eventually Roman power triumphed, and of the Venetic navy 'very few ships reached land in the gathering darkness.' In the operations which followed, we are told that Caesar showed no mercy to the rebels, but 'put the whole of their senate to the sword and sold the rest of the men as slaves.' The battle had been decisive and the rest of the year was spent in minor skirmishing in the north, culminating in the celebrated

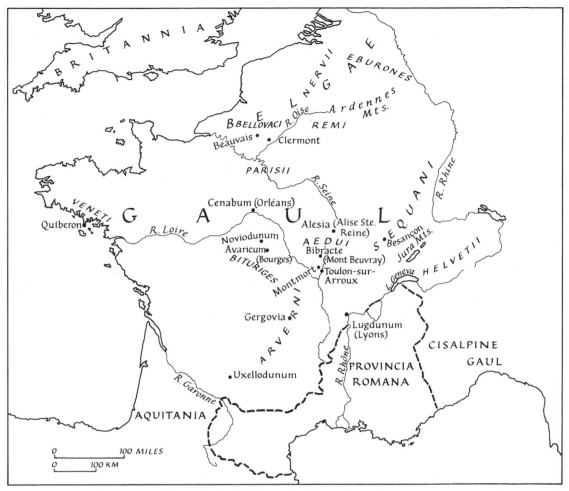

Gaul at the time of
Caesar's conquest.

crossing of the Rhine, the first time that Roman armies had pene-
trated the unknown territory beyond the river.

In the next two years Gaul was sufficiently quiet for Caesar to
turn his attention to Britain, where in 55 and 54 BC he conducted
limited campaigns of considerable risk and doubtful value. But all
was not well at base, for on his return to the continent in 54 he was
faced with a rebellion among the Eburones, in southern Belgium, led
by King Ambiorix. It took much of the next year to subdue the
revolt, in what was to prove one of the toughest and most brutal
campaigns of the entire war. The territory of the Eburones was
devastated, but Ambiorix escaped into the Ardennes.

The climax of the war came in 52 BC when the tribes of central
Gaul, who had so far remained uncommitted, finally rose up against
Rome under the inspiration of the great Arvernian war-leader
Vercingetorix. The revolt started with the slaughter of the Roman

merchants in the native *oppidum* of Cenabum. Caesar was in a difficult position, but retaliated by destroying the capital of the Bituriges
at Avaricum and then moved on to the town of Gergovia near
Clermont-Ferrand. There followed a terrible battle which resulted
in massive Roman losses, including forty-six centurions—the
NCO in charge of a unit of nominally 100 men, later to be reduced
to eighty. It was a near disaster and a dreadful blow for Caesar, but
for the rebels it spelt the beginning of a new hope: Caesar was not
invincible. Immediately people flocked to Vercingetorix's banner,
including the Aedui who until now had been faithful allies of Rome;
even Caesar's main supply depot at Noviodunum was captured. But
meanwhile one of Caesar's commanders, Labienus, had managed to
put down a rebellion of the Parisii in the Seine valley. Caesar now
made his way north to join him, with Vercingetorix in pursuit. The
armies met briefly, and after a short cavalry clash Vercingetorix made
his final fatal error—he withdrew to the defended hilltop of Alesia.
For Caesar it was the opportunity he had been awaiting. In a matter
of days the hill had been surrounded and the Roman army settled
down to starve the rebels out; and when a vast relieving force drawn
from all over Gaul arrived, Caesar was ready: in the ensuing battle
the Gallic army was destroyed and Vercingetorix, now without hope,
surrendered. After six years in a Roman prison he was eventually
put to death.

For Caesar it had been a tremendous success, but the war was
not quite over. Early in 51 the Belgic Bellovaci came out in open
revolt, but this was put down without much trouble, while further
south the *oppidum* of Uxellodunum formed a focus for further
resistance and had to be besieged. These events were, however,
little more than the last convulsion of Gaul's death agony—her
spirit had been smashed at Alesia. After a further year spent in
consolidation Caesar set out from *Gallia Comata* in the autumn
of 50 BC, never to return.

The story so briefly told loses much of its impact. The vast
distances over which the army marched, the weight of numbers
involved, the carnage on the battlefields, the squalor and the
disorder, all lurk behind the words of Caesar, but when his words
are strengthened by a knowledge of the actual ground, of the kind
provided by Colonel Stoffel and the archaeologists who followed
him, then something of the grim reality can be more readily sensed.
Here we can consider only a few of the more dramatic encounters.

No contemporary account gives a better idea of the tight cohesion

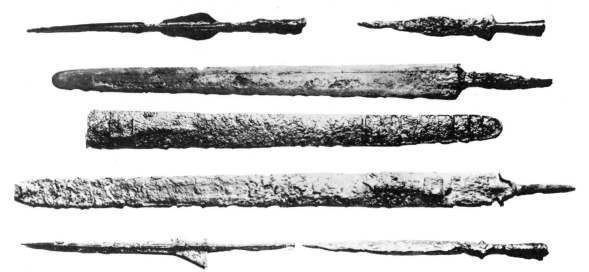

Iron weapons excavated at the battleground of Alesia.

of barbarian society than the story of the Helvetii as told by Caesar. As we have seen, it was their decision to migrate from their homeland in western Switzerland that gave Caesar his excuse to intervene in Gaulish affairs. Their territory was too small: they were hemmed in by natural barriers—the Rhine, the Jura Mountains, the Rhône and Lake Geneva. As the population grew they were forced to contemplate migration. This is how Caesar describes their preparations: they began 'by buying up all the draught cattle and wagons they could, sowing as much land as possible in order to secure an adequate supply of corn for the journey and establishing peaceful and friendly relations with their neighbours.' They thought that two years would be sufficient to complete their arrangements, then 'as soon as they considered themselves ready, they burnt all their twelve towns and four hundred villages, as well as the isolated buildings belonging to private individuals, and also their entire grain supply, except that which they intended to carry with them. For they thought that if there was no possibility of returning home, they would be more willing to face all the perils that awaited them. Every man was ordered to take from home three months' supply of flour for his own use.' Then, joined by a number of neighbours, they set out. It is a remarkable description of the care and thought that went into the preparation.

Of the two routes available to them, one lay through Roman territory, the other, much more difficult, across the land of the Sequani. They chose the former, but were forbidden to cross the Rhône by Caesar. Caesar tells us how he prepared to prevent any illegal crossing: 'He employed the legion he had with him . . . to fortify the bank of the Rhône for a distance of eighteen miles (28·9 kilometres) between Lake Geneva and the Jura . . . This was done by means of a rampart sixteen feet (4·88 metres) high with a ditch running parallel. He placed redoubts at intervals along the fortification and garrisoned them with pickets.' It need hardly be said that the indefatigable Colonel Stoffel, with his keen military sense, discovered three miles (4·8 kilometres) of the defensive line, together with four small forts along it, just as Caesar had described, all carefully sited to provide the best view of the river across which the attack was anticipated. The Colonel agreed that such a defence could easily have been held with the single legion and subsidiary troops at Caesar's disposal. Faced with this obstacle, the Helvetii made only one attempt to cross, then moved off to attempt to pass by the second route through the territory of the Sequani. After negotiation and an exchange of hostages the migrants were allowed through.

Then followed a period of negotiation, intrigue and minor engagements, until Caesar finally caught up with the main Helvetian force. The cat-and-mouse game was over, and Caesar prepared for the kill. By this stage the Roman army was close to the Helvetii and as an engagement seemed imminent, Caesar withdrew his troops to a nearby hillside, arranging his four veteran legions in three lines half-way up the hill. The two newly-recruited legions were stationed on the summit with all the auxiliaries, while the baggage packs were collected together in one place and defensive works dug around them. Battle commenced with the tightly-knit mass of Helvetii charging up the hill: 'By throwing down javelins from their commanding position the troops easily broke the enemy's phalanx, and then drew their swords and charged. The Gauls were much hampered in action because a single javelin often pierced more than one of their overlapping shields and pinned them together; and as the iron bent they could not pull them out. With their left arms thus encumbered, it was impossible for them to fight properly and many, after repeated attempts to jerk their shields free, preferred to drop them and fight unprotected. At length, exhausted by wounds, they began to fall back towards a hill about a mile away.' The battle raged furiously all day and until late into the night; at last the natives' stand behind their parked wagons was finally overcome. The survivors fled but were rounded up during the next few days.

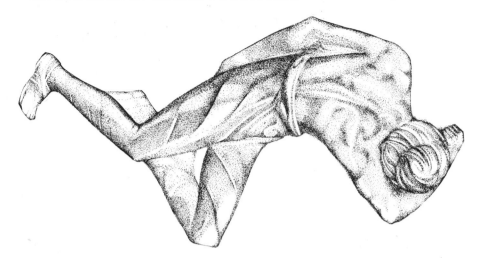

A dying Gaul.
Statuette four inches
in length from Alesia.

The actual site of the battle has been keenly debated. Stoffel, while working for Napoleon III, arrived at two possibilities. Napoleon plumped for one of them, but gradually Stoffel became more and more convinced that it was the other site, in a little valley at Montmort three miles (4·8 kilometres) north-west of Toulon-sur-Arroux. Finally he decided that the hill upon which Caesar deployed his troops must have been the hill of Armeçy. Excavation began in 1886 and three years later nine ditches arranged in a crescent shape were discovered. Not long after, pottery of the correct date turned up nearby. It is very tempting to agree with the Colonel that he had found the very earthwork which Caesar tells us was dug to protect his baggage on the day of the battle.

Something of the magnitude of the slaughter can be gauged from Caesar's closing remarks on the incident. Documents found by the victorious Romans in the Helvetian camp, written in Greek, 'contained a register of the names of all the emigrants capable of bearing arms, and also, under separate heads, the numbers of old men, women and children. The total was 368,000 . . . a census was taken of those who returned home: the number was found to be 110,000.'

For one of the last battles of the war Caesar's preparations were more extensive. In 51 BC, as we have seen, he moved against the Bellovaci. The native build-up seemed ominous, not least because the Belgic forces were negotiating for German reinforcements. For this reason Caesar decided to bring matters to a head. The natives believed he had only three legions at his disposal, whereas in fact he had four, but to encourage their mistake he arranged that three legions should march side by side in front, followed by the baggage train, with his fourth legion well to the back, not readily in sight. When the two armies were sufficiently close, Caesar set about building a particularly strong base camp on a hill overlooking the river behind which the Bellovaci had amassed. 'The Roman camp had a twelve-foot (3·66 metres) rampart with a breastwork of appropriate height, two ditches fifteen feet (4·57 metres) wide with vertical sides and three-storeyed towers at frequent intervals joined together by galleries protected by wicker breastwork . . . the gateways were fitted with doors and flanked with specially high towers.' One of the reasons for such elaborate defences was to make the camp so strong that it could be defended by a small force while the rest searched the countryside for food.

Between the two forces lay a marshy river valley, where skirmishes between foraging and raiding parties took place almost every day. Eventually, when he heard that reinforcements were close at hand, Caesar decided to advance: causeways were laid across the marsh and the legions crossed in safety to form a new camp on low ground below the native hilltop position. One night the rebels decided to retreat, having first lit a barrage of bonfires to confuse and frighten the Roman forces. 'This retreat, dictated by fear but executed with the utmost ingenuity, enabled them to reach, without any loss, a very strong position barely ten miles (16·1 kilometres) further on, where they encamped.' From there the Bellovaci planned an ambush, Roman forces were drawn into a clearing in the woods and then attacked. The plan seriously misfired: the natives were cut to pieces and their leader killed. Their defeat marked the end of the uprising, envoys were sent, peace terms agreed and the army eventually moved off.

Such a wealth of detail is given about Caesar's camp that it is only to be expected that it has been eagerly sought by generations of archaeologists. Napoleon of course claimed to have found it, at Mont St. Pierre, east of the River Oise, but the sides of the supposed Roman ditch were not vertical as Caesar described, and the site was later proved to be a native settlement. A few years later a local archaeologist came upon an ancient wooden bridge near Clermont, which he thought might be Caesar's bridge, but the discovery was not followed up and there the matter rested until in 1943 further evidence was published to suggest that Clermont (Oise) was, in fact, the site. On a low wooded plateau called Montagne de Nointel, 328 feet (100 metres) above the valley, it was claimed that Caesar's camp was discovered, preserved in detail. There were three separate camps enclosed together in an outer earthwork which defined an area of 250 acres. For part of the circuit the defences followed the irregular edge of the scarp, but where it cut across the plateau the rampart was set out in a series of straight lines. Inside were two large camps, each of about 55 acres, to house the legions, and a much smaller enclosure of about four acres where it is probable that Caesar's personal bodyguard was housed. Outside the main enclosure three auxiliary camps were found.

Down by the river, on the edge of the marshy valley of the River Brèche, the excavators found a forward defensive line, not described in the account of Caesar's activities. It consisted of a ditch, strengthened by sharpened jutting stakes, behind which was a palisade of upright timbers with the spaces between filled with wickerwork. At regular intervals behind this screen the troops had constructed eleven small fortlets each about half an acre in size to house patrol parties of about a hundred men. But more remarkable still were the two timber causeways which were found to cross the valley. One of these had been discovered in the 1860s but it was thought to be too elaborate to fit the contemporary description, which suggests that the bridges were laid very rapidly. If, however, the preparations had gone on for some time before in the lee of the palisade, the actual construction need not have taken long at all.

Each causeway was about 2,000 feet (610 metres) long and was constructed of bunches of brushwood pinned down into the subsoil;

Tentative reconstruction of Caesar's camp at Nointel, but see page 28 for doubts that have been cast on this location.

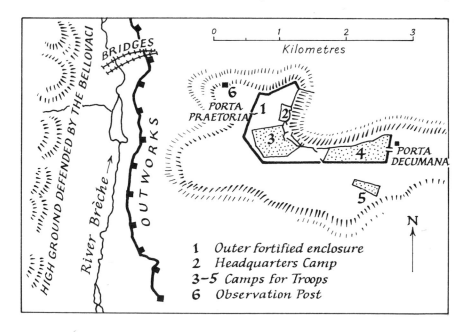

1 Outer fortified enclosure
2 Headquarters Camp
3–5 Camps for Troops
6 Observation Post

upon this base logs were laid, one course parallel to the line of the track, the next at right angles, the finished causeway being surfaced with sand. The two causeways start close together, but then diverge and run parallel so that two columns of troops could reach the enemy-held river bank together but some distance apart. Another refinement of the plan can be seen in the width of the causeways. They begin only twelve feet (3·66 metres) wide, but are increased in width in two stages until they reach a width of sixty feet (18·3 metres), sufficient for the soldiers to form up in a solid phalanx before reaching the enemy side.

It all sounds very convincing, but is it? In 1959 another French archaeologist published a paper in which he argued that the site did not fit Caesar's description and the remains were not Roman at all. There the matter rests—a splendid example of just how difficult it is, even today, to trace Caesar's footsteps.

Much the same uncertainty surrounded the identification of the famous site of Alesia where Vercingetorix made his last stand against the Romans in 52 BC, but most people now agree that it is Mont Auxois near the modern town of Alise Ste. Reine.

It is doubtful if for sheer impact and a feeling of immediacy it is possible to do better than look at the battle site of Alesia, and at the remarkable discoveries made by Colonel Stoffel in his two-year campaign of excavation.

The sequence of events must first be briefly told. The Gaulish cavalry had just been defeated and Vercingetorix withdrew to the hilltop stronghold of Alesia. Caesar says, 'It was clearly impregnable except to blockade: it stood at a high altitude on top of a hill washed by streams on the north and south and closely surrounded by other hills as high as itself on every side, except the west where a plain extended for some three miles. The whole slope below the town ramparts on the east was occupied by a camp crowded with Gallic troops who had fortified it with a ditch and a six-foot (1·83 metre) wall.' The only course open to Caesar was to lay siege: this he did by constructing an enclosing siege-work ten miles (16·1 kilometres) long with eight camps and twenty-three additional defended posts. For Vercingetorix the position was desperate: 80,000 people cooped up in Alesia had to be fed, and he realised that even with strict rationing his corn could only be made to last a month. His only hope was that reinforcements would arrive in time.

Caesar settled down for a long wait. Clearly, to protect his force from outside attack as well as to draw the line more strongly around

A model of Caesar's defensive system at Alesia, based on his own description.

the besieged Gauls, even more substantial defences were needed. 650 yards (594 metres) from one of his massive ditches he dug two further lines of ditches fifteen feet (4·57 metres) wide and in one place filled the inner one with water by diverting a stream. Behind these ditches he erected a palisaded rampart twelve feet (3·66 metres) high, with towers at intervals of 80 ft (24 metres). In the days that followed, furious attacks from the Gauls convinced him that even stronger defences were needed. Accordingly he added a further barrier of sharpened branches interlaced together and set in trenches projecting outwards towards the enemy—'Anyone who went among them was likely to impale himself on the sharp points.' In front, arranged in diagonal rows, were pits three feet (0·91 metres) deep, in the bottoms of which sharpened logs were embedded so as to project three inches (eight cms) above the ground. Earth was packed around their bases to keep them firm and the holes camouflaged with twigs and brushwood. These were in groups each containing eight rows three feet (0·91 metres) apart. The soldiers called them 'lilies' because of their similarity to the flower. Finally, in front of all this, wooden blocks with projecting iron points were embedded thickly in the ground. When all these defensive measures were completed, Caesar constructed a similar line facing outwards to protect his troops from attack from the rear: this line was fourteen miles (22·5 kms) long!

His caution was well justified, for news of the siege spread rapidly, with the result that a vast relieving force was soon amassed from all parts of Gaul numbering some quarter of a million troops under the overall command of Commius. It is not difficult to imagine the

Following Napoleon III's excavations, work continued on the Roman settlement that grew up on the hill of Alesia. This photograph of 1889 shows the excavated site.

effect the sight of the relief column must have had both on Caesar and Vercingetorix, as the motley multitude made camp on a hillside overlooking the plain, barely a mile from the Roman lines—delirious excitement among the besieged, matched by a calculated redeployment of troops by Caesar.

The engagement began with a cavalry battle from which the Romans emerged successful. A day later, under cover of darkness, the relieving army advanced towards the entrenchments on the plain. In the ensuing attack the effectiveness of Caesar's preparations soon made itself felt: 'As long as the Gauls were at a distance from the entrenchments, the rain of javelins which they discharged gained them some advantage, but when they came nearer they suddenly found themselves pierced on the iron spikes or tumbled into the pits and impaled . . . others were killed by heavy siege-spears discharged from the rampart and towers.' By dawn it was clear that the assault had failed and retreat followed.

The third attack was made on an outlying Roman camp to the north, outside the defensive earthworks. The fighting here was bitter and protracted: twice Roman relief columns had to be sent out, the second led by Caesar in person, while all this time the besieged Gauls, urged on by Vercingetorix, were attacking the Roman lines from within Alesia. Eventually, after some most ferocious fighting, the Gauls faltered, and in the rout which followed many thousands were slaughtered, even into the early hours of the next morning. The next day Vercingetorix surrendered and six years later he was ritually strangled in Rome in the aftermath of Caesar's triumph.

The identification of Alesia is beyond doubt Alise Ste. Reine. It was here in the 1860s that Napoleon's work force laboured so long to disentangle the complex of earthworks which Caesar had constructed almost 2,000 years before. Gradually the details became clearer—the hill of Alesia itself was surrounded by the long containing earthwork, making good defensive use of the streams which flanked the hill. Outside this circuit lay Caesar's outer defensive works, very carefully designed to include as much of the flanking hilltops as possible, to prevent the relieving force from making use of the high ground. It was here that four large infantry camps were discovered, together with some of the smaller command posts which Caesar mentions. Three more camps were found on the plain in front of the outer earthwork, facing the hill of Mussy-la-Fosse, where the Gaulish relief force set up its camp. But perhaps most dramatic of all were the finds on the southern slopes of Mont Réa,

Monument raised by
Napoleon III at
Alesia in honour of
the Gaulish war-
leader, Vercingetorix.

just north of the main defences—the site of the bloodiest of battles
which eventually turned into a hard-won Roman victory. Here the
excavators found an estimated five cubic metres of débris from the
battle, coins all minted not later than 52 BC, helmets, cuirasses,
spears, swords, shield bosses, spurs and *ballista* balls, all mixed up
with the bones of the horses and men who died in the onslaught.

On the west end of the hill of Alesia there now stands a vast
bronze statue, a noble male with flowing robes, long hair and drooping moustaches. It was erected in 1865 by Napoleon III to com-
memorate Vercingetorix's last stand against the forces of imperialism.
It cannot fail also to serve as a reminder of the archaeologist-
emperor himself, who five years later was to lose his own empire in
the disastrous Franco-Prussian War.

Caesar's conquest was complete: Gaulish energy and youth had
been consumed in eight years of gruelling fighting, their power to
resist was at an end. All that now remained was for the Roman ad-
ministrators to take over and convert the war-shattered territory
into a thriving and productive province of the Empire. Towns were
founded, some of them for veterans from the Roman armies,
members of the Gaulish aristocracy who had supported Rome
were rewarded, the Roman legal and administrative system was
imposed and Gaul under its new management settled back to enjoy
four hundred years of peace and prosperity. There were, admittedly,
minor setbacks: the Aquitani of western Gaul rebelled in 39–38
BC, and in 27 BC, when the Emperor Augustus visited the country to
supervise the first stages of a nationwide census, native resentment
ran high, but these were minor incidents in the otherwise smooth
path towards total Romanisation. The culmination came with the
dedication of a great altar to Rome and Augustus at Lugdunum
(Lyons) in 12 BC. Henceforth, once a year, the altar was to serve as a
focus for the great national assembly—the *Concilium Galliarum*—
which served to bind the disparate tribes of Gaul into a solid, powerful body, at one with Rome. In less than a lifetime the unruly 'hairy
Gauls' had settled into generations of respectability.

3

Nations Hitherto Unknown: Agricola in Scotland

After Caesar's expeditions of 55 and 54 BC, Rome made no serious attempt to gain control of Britain until AD 43, when the Emperor's legions once more sailed across the Channel to meet the native armies amassed in Kent. The initial advance was comparatively easy—the foremost native capital of Camulodunum (Colchester) was taken within the first few weeks (the troops led briefly by the Emperor Claudius himself), and by AD 47 most of the south-east of the country had been subdued.

It seems likely that Rome's initial plan was to occupy only the productive lowland area of the country behind a frontier zone which they created from Lincoln to Exeter, marked now by the famous Roman road called the Fosse Way. But gradually they were drawn out beyond, west into Wales by the constant threat of raids from the Welsh mountain tribes, and north, first into Yorkshire to support their native allies against anti-Roman dissidents, and finally into Scotland.

Scotland was conquered between AD 80 and 84 by the Roman army of occupation under the command of Gnaeus Julius Agricola, a native of southern Gaul. Agricola knew Britain well: at about the age of eighteen he had served in the province as a junior officer under Suetonius Paulinus, campaigning first in North Wales and later taking part in the awful carnage which followed the rebellion of Queen Boudicca. After this grim initiation he returned to Rome for a while to further his career, but was posted back to Britain about ten years later—this time as commander of the Twentieth Legion under the governor Petillius Cerialis. There followed a brief spell as governor of Aquitania (a province in what is now the western part of France) before he returned finally to Britain in AD 78 as governor of the island and commander-in-chief of its armies. At the age of thirty-eight he had reached a highly satisfactory position: now with four well seasoned legions and a host of auxiliaries at his call and the larger part of Britain still unconquered, he could use his position to create personal success.

Because of a happy coincidence of circumstances it is no exaggeration to say that we probably know more about Agricola's conquest of Scotland than about any other Roman campaign against barbarians. The circumstances are three: first, Agricola's daughter married the Roman historian Tacitus, who wrote an extremely full account of the general's campaigns, no doubt based on his own first-hand descriptions. Second, the army advanced over territory which until recently has been largely undisturbed by modern farming, where the skills of several extremely talented field workers and excavators could be brought to bear on well preserved structures such as marching camps and forts. And thirdly, lack of modern urban development has allowed the discovery of entirely unsuspected sites by air photography. In the pages that follow, we will look at these three quite different but entirely complementary approaches.

The actual survival of any work of ancient literature is a matter for surprise, particularly when it is realised how few copies were produced and how easy it was, in the turmoil following the collapse of Rome, for books to be destroyed. The early history of Tacitus's book, *Agricola*, is obscure, but somehow a manuscript copied from a late classical version in the ninth century survived in the monastery of Fulda in the German state of Hesse. There it remained unnoticed until the eleventh century when the historian Adam of Bremen paraphrased part of one of the chapters in his own work on the history of the church of Hamburg. Some sixty years later the librarian of the Abbey of Monte Cassino in Italy also quoted extensively from the *Agricola*. Could it be that two manuscripts survived? It is more likely that the Monte Cassino work was copied from the Fulda manuscript, since the two establishments are known to have had close links, and exchanges of literature were reasonably common.

It was not until the beginning of the fifteenth century that the world of scholarship began to take note of the manuscript treasures hidden away in German monasteries. The newly discovered works were much discussed, and after dealings of some obscurity the German version of Tacitus's *Agricola* reached Rome in about 1470: it was first printed five to ten years later in Milan and thenceforth became available to the world at large. How many hundreds of editions have subsequently been published it is impossible to say.

The story which Tacitus tells is naturally a biased one: both he and his father-in-law were liberal men accustomed to the tradition of freedom and good government which prevailed during the reign of the Emperor Vespasian (69–79). For Tacitus the *Agricola* served two purposes: it enabled him to pay homage to the achievements of Agricola, for whom he clearly had a high respect, while at the same time it provided a vehicle for offering criticism of the repressive reign of the Emperor Domitian (81–96). In other words, it played down the successes of Agricola's predecessors and was something of a political tirade as well. But in spite of all this it tells its story with remarkable clarity.

Agricola had been in Britain, campaigning in North Wales and northern England, for a year and a half before the south could be regarded as sufficiently stable to allow him to turn his attention to the virtually unknown territory of Scotland. It was in the third summer that he crossed the Tyne and Edin into the territory of the Selgovae and Votadini (now south-eastern Scotland) and pushed forward as far north as the River Tay. Adverse weather conditions made the advance difficult, but there seems to have been very little native resistance. The next year was wisely spent in 'securing the districts already overrun' and planting a number of garrisons in forts along the narrow neck of land between the inlets of the Clyde and Forth— the line which was later chosen to be the frontier—a continuous turf rampart and ditch garrisoned by forts—constructed by the Emperor Antoninus. As Tacitus says, 'The enemy had been pushed into what was virtually another island.'

In the next year, AD 82, Agricola turned his attention to the south-west of Scotland occupied by a tribe called the Novantae who were hitherto unknown to the Romans. When the task was complete he must have stood on the western shores and looked across to Ireland thinking of further territorial gains, if only men and time would allow. Tacitus says he had often heard Agricola claim that Ireland could have been conquered and held by a single legion and a few auxiliaries. It is tempting to think of the old man sitting back in Rome in later years, telling his guests stories of his exploits in Britain and wistfully reminiscing about the battles he would have liked to have fought.

Three seasons in southern Scotland had been sufficient to stabilise the entire territory south of the Forth-Clyde line; now the final

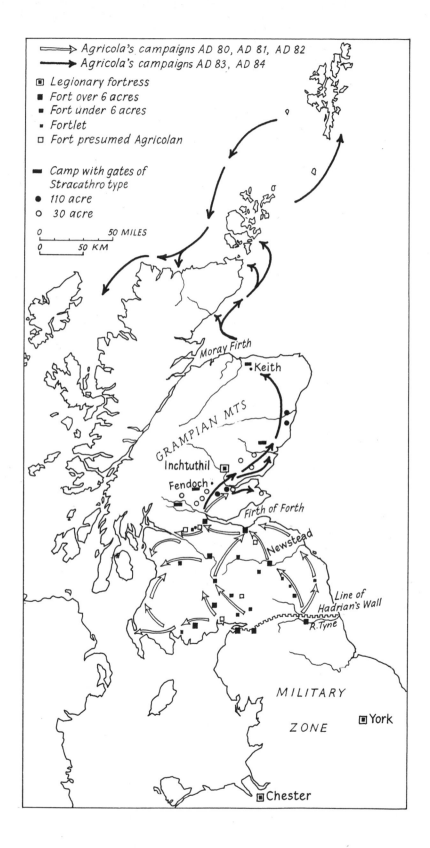

Agricola's campaigns
in Scotland

Legend (within map):

→ Agricola's campaigns AD 80, AD 81, AD 82
→ Agricola's campaigns AD 83, AD 84
▣ Legionary fortress
■ Fort over 6 acres
■ Fort under 6 acres
▪ Fortlet
□ Fort presumed Agricolan

▬ Camp with gates of Stracathro type
● 110 acre
○ 30 acre

0   50 MILES
0   50 KM

Moray Firth
Keith
GRAMPIAN MTS
Inchtuthil
Fendoch
Firth of Forth
Newstead
Line of Hadrian's Wall
R. Tyne
MILITARY ZONE
York
Chester

advance could begin. Geography drastically influenced the form of the campaign. The Highlands were a potential death trap, and Agricola must have decided at the outset not to let his troops be drawn into the glens where ambush would have been so easy. Instead, the army marched along the eastern coastal plain, making good use of the sea and rivers to bring up supplies of men and arms. 'The war was pushed forward simultaneously by land and sea; the infantry, cavalry and marines often meeting in the same camp would eat together and celebrate.'

It was now, at the height of the Roman success, that the native resistance began to gain cohesion. Instead of retreating before the Romans, they took the offensive and attacked a Roman fort. To some of the Romans the situation seems to have appeared serious enough to suggest that a dignified retreat behind the Forth was called for, but as events turned out the Romans stood their ground, regrouped and eventually managed to advance. The Britons were not dismayed, and as a counter-measure they decided on a night assault on the camp of the Ninth Legion. They killed the sentries and managed to break in before Agricola's scouts reached him with news of the attack. By dawn his entire army had reached the camp and were engaged in counter-attacking the enemy's rear. Caught between the two armies the Britons gave up and fled into the safety of the forests and marshes. It had been a difficult moment for the Romans and a timely reminder that they were still by no means masters of the country.

In the next (and last) year of his governorship, Agricola prepared for the final confrontation. While the Britons were amassing under the leadership of their war leader, Calgacus, he sent the fleet forward to plunder and cause havoc while the army marched towards the scene of what was to be the last great battle—the battle of Mons Graupius. Tacitus describes the order of battle in some detail. On the Roman side the troops were carefully arranged. The legionaries were kept in reserve outside the rampart of the Roman camp, where they would be readily available if required. In front were the troops of the first wave, 8,000 auxiliary infantry in the centre with 3,000 cavalry divided between the flanks. The Britons were assembled on higher ground in tiers so as to impress—there were some 30,000 of them—while in the space between the two armies the British aristocracy drove furiously up and down in their chariots, no doubt hurling abuse at the enemy in true Celtic manner and boasting of their own prowess.

As usual the fighting began with an exchange of missiles and then, strictly according to accepted practice, Agricola sent forward six auxiliary cohorts of Batavi and Tungri (from the Rhine mouth region) to engage in hand-to-hand fighting. Tacitus takes up the narrative: 'The manoeuvre was . . . most inconvenient to the enemy with their small shields and unwieldy swords—swords without a thrusting point, and therefore unsuited to the clash of arms in close fighting. The Batavi began to rain blow after blow, push with the bosses of their shields and stab at their enemies in their faces. They routed the enemy on the plain and pushed on uphill. This provoked the rest of our cohorts to drive in hard and butcher the enemy as they met him. Many Britons were left behind half dead or even unwounded, such was the speed of our victory.' Meanwhile the cavalry, having dealt with the war chariots, joined in the main battle.

The British reserves now tried an outflanking movement, but this was repelled by a small detachment of cavalry which Agricola had kept back. Next it was the Roman turn to try to outflank the enemy, with a notable degree of success: 'The spectacle that followed over the open country was awe-inspiring and grim. Our men followed hard, took prisoners and then killed them . . . on the enemy's side . . . some bands, though armed, fled before inferior numbers, some men, though unarmed, insisted on charging to their deaths. Weapons, bodies, severed limbs, lay all around, and the earth reeked of blood.'

As the battle died down, the magnitude of the victory began to be appreciated. In the final summing up it was claimed that 10,000 Britons had died for the loss of only 360 on the Roman side: 'The next day revealed the quality of the victory more distinctly. A grim silence reigned on every hand, the hills were deserted, only here and there was smoke seen rising from chimneys in the distance, and our scouts found no one to encounter them.' The battle was over and Britain lay conquered. Agricola could now pass over a peaceful province to his successor and return to Rome.

The bare bones of Tacitus's narrative, summarised here, with all its bias, conformity to accepted style and lack of geographical precision, is still marvellous material from which to work. How many times, one wonders, are the phrases used by Tacitus half-remembered echoes of the general's actual words as he relived once more the glories of the past for the benefit of his attentive biographer? But given the narrative, given the open countryside of Scotland with its great archaeological potential, one more ingredient was needed before the two could be brought together in harmony—an archaeologist with a rare combination of dogged determination, brilliant insight and meticulous attention to detail. Such a man was Ian Archibald Richmond.

Ian (later Sir Ian) Richmond was born in Rochdale and educated in Classics at Oxford, where he was taught by the remarkable philosopher-archaeologist, R. G. Collingwood. While still at Oxford he took part in what can fairly be called the first of the modern excavations, at the Roman fort of Segontium, now Carnarvon in North Wales, under the direction of Mortimer Wheeler. Suitably initiated into the fine art of excavation, he embarked upon a long and distinguished career, excavating in Britain and working in the British School at Rome, of which he was to become director for a short period. Eventually in 1935 he took up a post as lecturer in the University of Newcastle, where he stayed until his final move to Oxford in 1956 as Professor of the Archaeology of the Roman Empire. Throughout his varied working life, Richmond's energies were concentrated upon the military archaeology of Roman Britain. From Newcastle he was admirably placed to follow his consuming interest both in the great military complex of Hadrian's Wall and in other remains beyond it in Scotland. How could a scholar so placed and so motivated have failed to respond to the challenge of Agricola's campaigns? Richmond's response was immediate.

He already knew Scotland well; indeed as an undergraduate at Oxford he had published a long discussion of the geography of Scotland as recorded by the ancient geographer Ptolemy. Now he sat back and reviewed the evidence afresh. Many forts had been dug into in Scotland, some had produced fragments of pottery dating to the Agricolan period, but practically nothing was known of what a fort of this period was like. Clearly what was needed was the thorough excavation of an Agricolan fort uncluttered by later rebuilding. The fort he finally chose was Fendoch in Perthshire, a strongpoint so sited as to guard the mouth of the Sma' Glen which leads into the Highland massif. The remains at Fendoch seem to have first been discovered by Colonel Shand in 1788, but were lost sight of until Richmond and his co-worker, James McIntyre, rediscovered them in the course of field work in 1936.

Excavation took place in 1936 and '37 and the results were promptly published in the next year. Richmond's method of working was small scale: he liked to oversee all the digging in detail

Ian Richmond explains the gate at Fendoch to the great Scottish archaeologist, Sir George Macdonald (*right*).

himself, which meant employing a small group of local workers, each of whom was personally supervised. Unlike what happens on modern excavations, in which large areas are totally stripped, Richmond preferred to dig narrow trial trenches, carefully and thoughtfully placed to give the maximum amount of information for the minimum expenditure of energy. The ramparts of the fort were tested in five complete sections and four trial holes, and two of the four gates were extensively excavated. The examination of the interior showed particular economy of effort: in the central block a number of trial pits and trenches were cut to trace the plan of each of the timber buildings, but in the two flanking blocks, where the barrack buildings were sited, the plans were recovered with a single long trial trench across each area, to demonstrate the positions of the individual structures, followed by a few trial holes sited so as to check the end walls and some of the corners. The result was that, in two short seasons, the plan of an Agricolan fort had, for the first time, been firmly established.

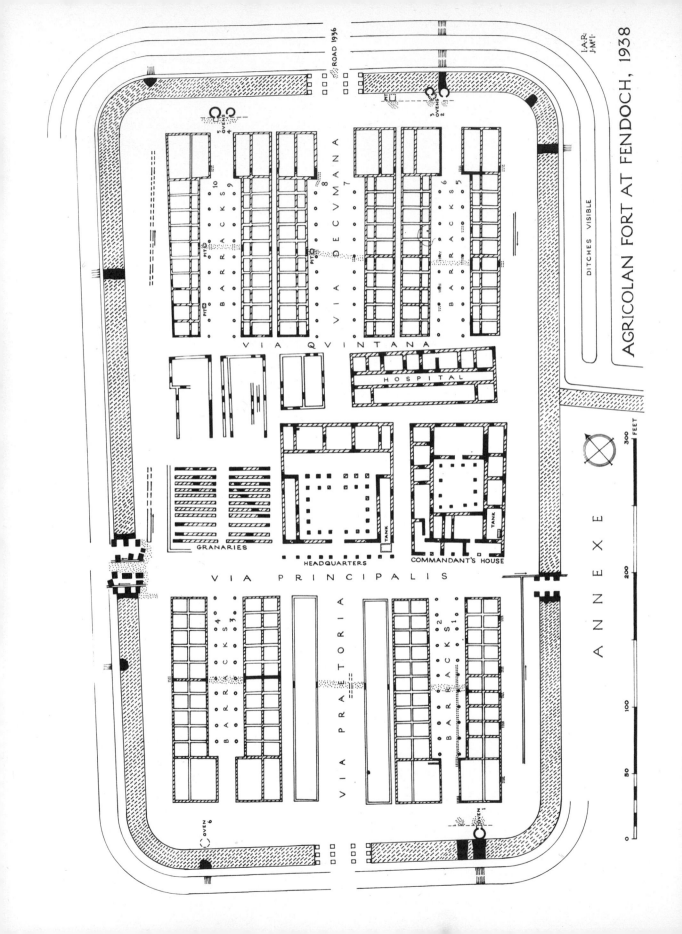

AGRICOLAN FORT AT FENDOCH, 1938

Sir Ian Richmond's own plan of his excavation at Fendoch. Most of the plan is a reconstruction based on trial trenches and pits. The positions of these can be traced because the walls exposed by them are shown in solid black.

The fort measured only 600 feet (183 metres) by 330 feet (100 metres), and was defended by a single turf rampart and ditch with a second ditch on the east side. Of the four gates, three were flanked with guard towers, which Richmond was able carefully to reconstruct, while the fourth was a simple opening leading into an annexe. The interior was divided into three equal-sized blocks by two roads, the *via principalis* and the *via quintana*. In the first (front) block, known as the *praetentura*, were two pairs of barrack blocks facing each other, each pair flanked by long sheds, probably kit-stores; while in the equivalent position at the back of the fort, the *retentura*, were six barracks of similar type. Each barrack consisted of ten rooms with ante-rooms facing on to a continuous verandah. Each set of rooms represented a Roman mess-unit of eight men called a *contubernium*—the group who on the march would share a single tent. At the end of each range was a larger set of rooms for the centurion, while just beyond, set into the back of the rampart, were the ovens where the men would prepare their food, sufficiently far away from their timber buildings to remove the risk of fire. The barrack building, then, represented a military unit known as a century, which at this time was composed of eighty men. The existence of ten barracks showed that the fort was designed to house a *cohors milliaria peditata*—an infantry unit of auxiliaries nominally of a thousand men, but in actual fact a little over eight hundred strong.

In the central block lay the principal buildings of the fort, the headquarters (*principia*), and the commander's house (*praetorium*). The headquarters was, of course, the centre of the life of the fort: it contained a courtyard flanked by the armouries, a cross-hall with its tribunal for use when courts-martial were being heard, and beyond, a range of five offices to house the pay chest, the standards, the cohort's records and the unit's shrine.

Next to the headquarters was a pair of granaries (*horrea*), which Richmond estimated were sufficiently large to hold a full year's supply of corn for the troops, with a little left over. Nearby he found cart sheds and store buildings, and finally, behind the commander's house, the hospital with a long consulting room and ten small wards, one for each century. Again Richmond turned bare archaeological fact into human terms by pointing out that since each room would take only four beds, the anticipated casualty rate was at about the five per cent level. His life-long interest in Roman military medicine may perhaps owe something to the fact that his father had been a medical practitioner.

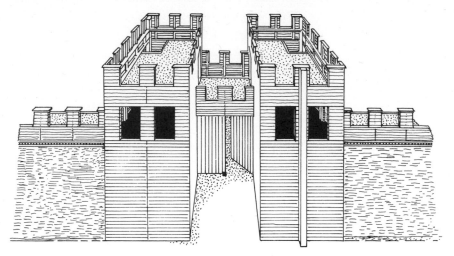

Reconstruction of the gate of Agricola's fort at Fendoch.

Fendoch still serves to give fascinating insight into life in Agricola's army in the early 80s at a time when plans were being laid to establish a permanent holding force in Scotland. Forts like Fendoch were carefully placed so as to prevent any build-up of natives in the mountains using the glens as routes to attack Agricola's supply lines along the flanking plain. It was the garrison's function to observe, patrol and above all to serve as a restraint to native movements. What the feelings of those eight hundred men crammed together in isolation in a remote part of the Scottish landscape must have been, we can only guess.

Apart from the intensely vivid insight into military conditions which the excavation of Fendoch gave, the excavation served as a model: never before had such skill been shown in the excavation of timber military structures. The great field archaeologist, O. G. S. Crawford, was particularly impressed. Writing a few years after the excavation, in 1943, he picked out a small detailed observation for comment: Richmond's reconstruction-drawing of the gate showed it covered with weather-boarding. No timber survived but the boarding was not pure conjecture, for it was inferred from the fact that where the turves, which had fallen from the rampart, abutted the gate-tower, they were found to end in a vertical line representing the position of the since-rotted boards. Such an observation would occasion no surprise nowadays, but thirty years ago the science of excavating timber-work was still in its infancy. Crawford concluded his comments by saying, 'I stress these facts because the achievements of modern excavating techniques are still little known; they have advanced far ahead of the possibilities of using them in a country which is still dominated by a bookish and clerical conception of culture'—an unkind but possibly justified comment on the sad state of Scottish archaeology which Richmond's work did so much to improve.

In 1952 Richmond returned once more to the problems of the Agricolan campaign, this time in the company of Dr J. K. St Joseph, well known not only for his study of Roman military installations but also for his pioneering work in the field of aerial photography. Together, each September for fourteen years, they carefully dissected Agricola's great legionary fortress at Inchtuthil, in Perthshire. Only a few days after the completion of the final season, Richmond died.

Inchtuthil lies on an isolated plateau on the north bank of the River Tay. It had been known since the fifteenth century but was dismissed by the early antiquarians as a Pictish town burnt at the time of the Roman conquest. A desultory excavation, characteristic of the time, had been carried out by the Society of Antiquaries of Scotland in 1901, the results of which were more intelligibly interpreted by Sir George Macdonald eighteen years later, by which time the old trenches had been largely overgrown and a fine bath house, which had been excavated and left open, had become a 'melancholy spectacle of desolation and decay'. But sufficient survived for Macdonald to interpret the site as the winter quarters of a small army which he assigned to the Agricolan period. It was Richmond, in his first publication as an undergraduate, who identified the site as *Pinnata Castra*, recorded in Greek by Ptolemy, a name denoting a legionary fortress defended by a breastwork with parapets placed upon the ramparts. Thirty years were to elapse before the true nature of the site began to emerge.

Although the final report on this vitally important site has still to be published, we do have the benefit of short interim reports prepared annually after each season's work and published in the *Journal of Roman Studies*. The fortress covered 53 acres and was defended by a single turf bank and ditch, the bank being later strengthened with a stone wall five feet (1·52 metres) thick. The gates, like those of Fendoch, were of timber, consisting of massive towers, but this time flanking dual carriageway approach roads. In the interior, a vast complex of timber buildings gradually came to light—here indeed was a legionary fortress unique in its completeness. No fewer than 64 large barracks provided accommodation for the troops, whose senior officers lived in four spacious tribunes' houses, each more substantial than the commandant's house at Fendoch. The fortress was planned to accommodate about 6,000 men.

There were six large granaries, an aisled drill-hall, a construction shop where equipment was made and repaired, a huge hospital constructed in the form of a hollow square with wards opening off either side of a continuous corridor, and a centrally-sited headquarters building. The roads were for the most part lined with continuous colonnades behind which were arranged 180 store-rooms. Outside the fortress the excavators found the temporary camp used by the builders, a stores compound and a separate residential compound for the senior officers in charge of building operations.

Quite clearly a work of this magnitude could not have been constructed in a short period. The acquisition of sufficient seasoned timber alone must have required much detailed planning and considerable organisational ability. In fact Inchtuthil provides an excellent example of work in progress. The programme was sufficiently far advanced for the fortress to have provided all the accommodation required for the troops (indeed, the builders' camp had been abandoned) but many of the ovens showed no sign of having been used, and there were still open spaces within the defences requiring development. At least two more tribunes' houses and probably two more granaries were to be erected and work had not yet begun on the commander's house or legate's palace, although the space for them had been reserved next to the headquarters. Outside, in the residential compound, the structure of the bath house had been completed, but the hot-water system remained to be installed. All this Richmond carefully deduced from a meticulous and thoughtful observation of even the smallest detail.

While it cannot be doubted that the work was unfinished, the fact that the turf rampart had been cut back and a thick stone wall added is an indication that plans were changing during building. It gives the impression that after work had started the decision was taken that the legion was here to stay. But military policies change rapidly: within three or four years of building having been begun, the order to abandon the fortress and withdraw was suddenly given.

Here again Richmond's powers of observation and interpretation fill in the detail. Everywhere he found evidence that the principal timbers of the gates and buildings had been carefully uprooted, presumably in order to be returned to store: nails pulled out with claw-hammers had been discarded in the foundation trenches and timber cladding and infill material were gathered into heaps for

OPPOSITE
Sir Ian Richmond's plan of the legionary fortress at Inchtuthil. Compare with the aerial photograph on page 50.

INCHTUTHIL : GENERAL PLAN OF THE LEGIONARY FORTRESS

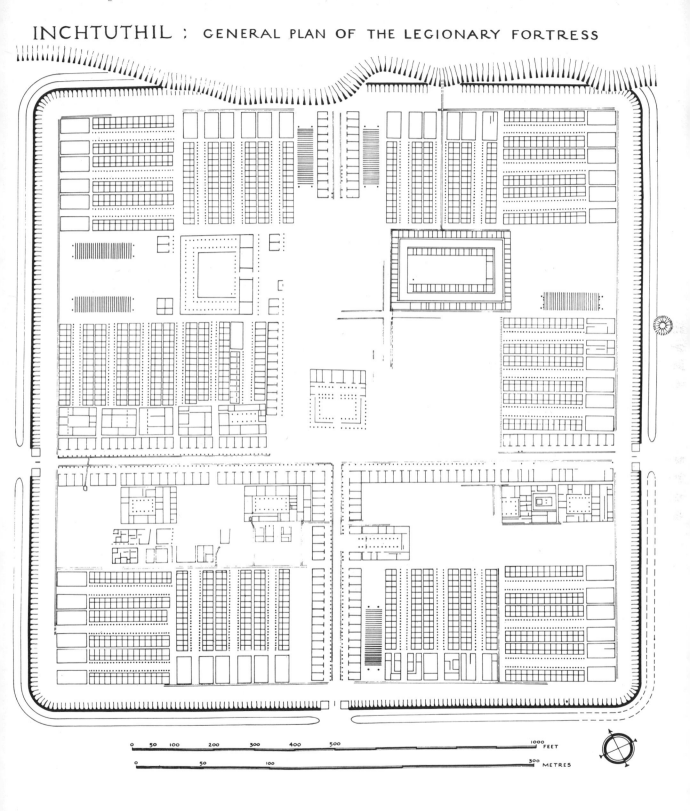

| 0 | 50 | 100 | 200 | 300 | 400 | 500 | | 1000 | FEET |

| 0 | | 50 | | 100 | | 300 | METRES |

OPPOSITE
Celtic god from
Bouray (Seine et
Marne). The figure is
made from a single
sheet of bronze,
beaten out from
behind. He wears a
torc typical of Celtic
aristocratic dress.
Height 16½ inches
(420 mm).

burning. The stonework was also carted off: the blocks of the fortress wall were taken down, the stone drains uprooted, while in the residential compound walls were removed, flue-tiles stripped off and stone flagging prised up. But perhaps most remarkable of all was the discovery, in the construction shop, of a pit where about one million iron nails of all sizes had been dumped, presumably to prevent the iron from falling into the hands of the enemy who might convert it into weapons. The evidence for orderly demolition is both convincing and complete.

The discovery of freshly minted bronze coins of AD 86 or 87 in destruction levels is proof that the abandonment came after Agricola had left the province. Now Tacitus specifically states that following Agricola's return to Rome, Britain was 'let slip'. To understand why, we must briefly consider what was happening outside Britain. In 86–7 the Roman legions stationed on the Danube were disastrously defeated by the Dacians (see Chapter 4). To re-establish control, it was necessary to draft in substantial reinforcements for the counter-offensive which was to be mounted in 88, and one of the legions transferred at this time was the Second *Adiutrix*, which had hitherto been at Chester. To move a whole legion from this key position, dividing the tribes of Wales from those of the Pennines, without sending replacements, would have been unthinkable, and since the only legion to spare was the Twentieth, now in Scotland and preparing to move into its new fortress of Inchtuthil, the inevitable course had to be taken: the Twentieth was recalled to Chester and Agricola's plan for the permanent occupation of Scotland had to be abandoned. Thus Richmond's carefully observed evidence of demolition at both Inchtuthil and at Fendoch fits neatly with the known historical facts. Agricola's plan to occupy the vale of Strathmore was set to one side. The army settled down to the south of the Clyde-Forth line, while the northern barbarians moved down from the Highlands to regroup once more as a threat to the stability of the province.

Sufficient will have been said to give some idea of Ian Richmond's contribution to the problems posed by Agricola's campaigns. By well chosen and thorough research excavation, he was able to give a new clarity and immediacy to the narrative of Tacitus, but to offer greater geographical precision a different technique was required—that of aerial photography. For more than thirty years Dr J. K. St Joseph, Professor of Aerial Photography at Cambridge, has been flying over the territory of Scotland, tracing the routes

Above Coins of Julius Caesar and of his Gaulish opponent, Vercingetorix. *Below* The insignia of the Gaulish Legion, formed after the Roman conquest of Gaul. Figures of boars were particularly common in the religious art of pre-Roman Gaul.

Aerial photograph of marching camp at Stracathro. Although the ditch has been completely filled with soil, its position can be traced because the crop above it grows taller and ripens later. In the photograph it shows as a thin dark line. The peculiar arrangement of the ditches at the gate can be seen in the centre foreground.

of the various Roman campaigns fought and re-fought over this stretch of the countryside. Although the work is still far from complete, a bewildering variety of new camps have been discovered, which on the ground would have been totally unrecognisable. Gradually St Joseph is unpicking the threads and laying out for us groups of camps which are likely to have resulted from a single season's campaign.

Here we must make the distinction between the permanently occupied forts like Fendoch, with their substantial and recognisable ramparts and ditches, and the temporary camps, constructed by the army on the march where, for a night or two, they could pitch their tents in relative safety. The ditches of this type of fortification could be as little as five feet (1·52 metres) across and two feet (0·61 metres) deep, just sufficient to provide a bank of soil in which the stakes carried by the soldiers could be embedded to create a temporary palisade. Such insubstantial structures would rapidly be obliterated by weathering and later farming activities. Whereas the forts provide the information needed to understand how Agricola planned to hold Scotland, the camps show us how he set about conquering it in the first place. To gain the complete picture we need both kinds of evidence.

Professor St Joseph can now recognise five different sets of

Aerial photograph of Inchtuthil. The line of the defences shows clearly, but under the conditions of light and crop prevailing no trace of the internal buildings appears.

marching camps. Four are distinguishable by their size, averaging 30 acres, 63 acres, 110 acres and 130 acres: the fifth, which he calls after the site of Stracathro, is also about 30 acres in area but is distinguished by a very distinctive form of entrance constructed by out-turning the bank and ditch on either side of the entrance passage, one arm being straight and oblique to the camp wall, the other curving out to meet it. Why such a peculiar arrangement was adopted is difficult to say, but it is tempting to suggest that it represented the preference of a particular military engineer. Of these five types, each presumably representing different campaigns, the 63-acre and 130-acre can be shown to relate to a later military advance under the Emperor Severus and do not concern us here: the other three types however must have been constructed during Agricola's campaigns.

The two types of 30-acre camp were each sufficient to house a single legion on the march. Since we know that Agricola had at his disposal considerably more than one legion, and on one occasion was actually marching in three divisions, it could well be argued that the different types of camp represent the progress of different campaigning units. Professor St Joseph goes on to reinforce the argument by pointing out that nowhere do the two types occur together and the shortest distance between any two is five and three-quarter miles (9·2 kilometres): in fact the distributions are different but reinforce each other, just as one would expect of an army advancing in separate columns. The 110-acre camps can best be regarded as the work of the entire army marching together, quite possibly in the last year's campaign which culminated in the battle of Mons Graupius.

Gradually then, through excavation and fieldwork following upon intensive aerial survey, the details of Agricola's campaigns are becoming clearer; but where was the final battle of Mons Graupius fought? Sir George Macdonald believed that the Roman force had been firmly established at Inchtuthil in the final year and therefore the battle must have taken place somewhere north of the Tay. Richmond was more precise, suggesting that Calgacus made his last stand when the Romans began to threaten the rich plains of the Moray Firth and therefore the battle must have been sited somewhere in the Pass between Auchinhove and Keith. More recently, however, the suggestion has been put forward that it was actually fought south of the Tay near Duncrab, but this too has been proved incorrect.

About the battlefield, then, there is no certainty, and it is unlikely that there ever will be. Napoleon III had the massive siege-works of Caesar to guide him to Alesia, but the battle of Mons Graupius was over in a day. Apart from the Roman camp and the graves of those who died in the slaughter, little archaeological trace is likely to have survived. But just possibly, one day, by accident or design, some hint of where the Britons' last stand took place may come to light.

4

Rome beyond the Danube: Trajan and Decebalus

The story of Rome's expansion into Europe was dominated by her need to discover and establish logical and defensible frontiers. In Britain, although economic considerations suggested limited occupation of the lowlands behind the Fosse frontier, pressures from outside drew the armies further into the unknown until Agricola's ships had reached Orkney. So it was in mainland Europe; by the time of Augustus (27 BC to AD 14), however, the frontiers had become more or less stabilised along the two great rivers, the Rhine and the Danube. Although some attempts had been made to push further north and east across Germany towards the River Elbe, they came to nothing.

The last major campaigns of conquest in Europe were fought over a mountainous tract of country beyond the north bank of the Danube—the territory of the Dacians. It was a clash of wills between the rapidly emerging civilisation of the Dacians, led by their king Decebalus, and the Roman Emperor Trajan (AD 98–117), hungry for military glory and with a shrewd eye on the renowned silver and gold deposits of Dacia. Trajan was the last of the aggressive Roman imperialist emperors. Admittedly, one of his successors, Marcus Aurelius (161–180), made some attempt to conquer still more of northern Europe, the lands of the Sarmatians and the Marcomanni, but this was in response to barbarian attack and the outcome was a failure. The death of Trajan in AD 117 can fairly be said to mark the end of Roman expansion.

Trajan was a remarkable leader, a typical tough Roman soldier who balked at nothing, but whereas Caesar's judgements were always reasoned and well considered, one cannot help feeling that

OPPOSITE
The forum of Trajan
in Rome, the setting
for Trajan's Column.

with Trajan there was just a touch of megalomania. His Dacian campaigns were, as we will see, well justified, but why in the latter part of his life did he embark on the fantastic enterprise of conquering Mesopotamia? He is said to have stood on the shores of the Red Sea and looked towards India, dreaming of further conquest. Some people suggest that he was suffering from delusions of grandeur, perhaps even believing himself to be a reincarnation of the Greek general Alexander the Great. There were similarities: above all he was a brilliant leader of soldiers, he loved his army and willingly shared their hardships, and it was under his guidance that the Roman military machine reached its most effective form.

Trajan fought two campaigns against the Dacians, the first from 101 to 102 and the second from 105 to 106. Like Caesar he wrote commentaries on the wars, but they have not survived, nor have any other major accounts: we have only fragments embodied in the works of later writers. It is therefore impossible to reconstruct the actual events in anything like the detail of Caesar's or Agricola's campaigns. However, another far more vivid source of evidence survives—Trajan's Column.

Trajan was a great monumentaliser; he loved building and in particular he liked to embellish his capital city with fine new structures. In the years following his Dacian campaigns, and no doubt using the spoils extracted from the new province to pay the costs, he employed his master builder, Apollodorus, to build a great new forum in Rome between the Capitoline and Quirinal hills. Apollodorus began by creating a level square three hundred feet (91 metres) across, which entailed cutting back a spur of the Quirinal Hill until the excavation was a hundred feet (30 metres) deep. Upon this new site the Basilica (law courts) of Trajan was built with two libraries, one for Latin works and one for Greek. The forum itself was surrounded by a colonnade, entered from the direction of the forum of Augustus through a monumental archway heavily embellished with sculpture. Between the two wings of the library stood Trajan's Column, a hundred feet (30 metres) high and covered with a continuous spiral band of reliefs depicting scenes from the Dacian wars. If the spiral band were unravelled it would measure 645 feet (196 metres) in length! On the base of the Column is an inscription which tells us that it was erected in AD 113 to represent the depth of material removed before the forum could be built.

Looking at the Column now, with its figures weathered by exposure, glowing white in the sunlight, it is difficult to remember that

originally it would have been highly coloured, with the spears and bows and arrows of the soldiers, made separately in bronze and attached to the marble, still further enhancing the vigour and energy of the design. Viewed at different levels from the windows of the libraries, it must have been a constant reminder of Roman strength to later generations. The dramatic effect of such a construction was not lost on another great general, Napoleon I; he copied the idea to illustrate the activities of his own Grand Army on the Vendôme Column, erected in Paris between 1806 and 1810.

Generations of scholars have looked at the reliefs on Trajan's Column in the hope that they would be able to use them to reconstruct the history of the two Dacian campaigns, but it is now generally agreed that the different scenes are not in strict chronological order. They do, however, give a brilliant insight into the activities of the army. How could such accuracy of detail have been attained? The most satisfactory suggestion is that a war artist accompanied Trajan during the campaigns and made detailed sketches of the events and scenes he saw. These field note-books were later worked into a continuous composition which the sculptors in Rome faithfully copied in stone. In modern terms it is rather as though a war correspondent's despatches were lost but his photographs survived.

If Trajan's Column were all that remained to tell us what the Dacian wars were like, we would be lucky, but there is actually far more; scraps of historical evidence, other monuments, roadworks, and the results of recent excavations of native sites by Romanian archaeologists. Moreover, discoveries are still being made. In the following pages we must attempt to bring some of these threads together to see what they can tell us of these eventful years in the first decade of the second century.

The Danube formed a magnificent natural frontier to Roman expansion. To the south and west, on the 'Roman' side, loose military control had been established by the time the Emperor Augustus died in AD 14. At Arrabona in Hungary, an auxiliary fort was established on the Danube bank, while further west at Carnuntum in Austria a legion had been moved up into position on the river. There was no need at this stage for massive frontier works or troop concentrations, because the normal Roman policy was adopted of entering into treaty relations with the tribes to the north so as to form buffers against any attacks from beyond. This, at any event, was the policy which Augustus initiated, and for a while it worked, but

The first scenes on the base of Trajan's Column. The army crosses the Danube on a bridge constructed of boats watched over by the river god.

gradually more troops were moved up to stations along the river. Then in AD 85 the Dacians, whose strength was rapidly increasing, attacked the Roman province of Moesia. There had been troubles from the northern tribes a few years earlier in 69, but these were minor compared with the initial onslaughts of the Dacians in 85. They burst through the Roman defences into the province, causing great havoc and killing the governor. For the Emperor Domitian the situation was very serious, and it was partly for this reason that the Second *Adiutrix* Legion was withdrawn from Britain. Domitian attended to the war in person at first but eventually he passed control of the operation to Cornelius Fuscus. The province of Moesia was soon cleared and in 87 Fuscus began campaigning in eastern Dacia, but once the Romans were in enemy territory the might of the Dacian forces began to tell. Gradually the Roman army was driven back and in a devastating battle virtually the entire force was annihilated and Fuscus himself was killed.

Where the slaughter took place is not known for certain, but

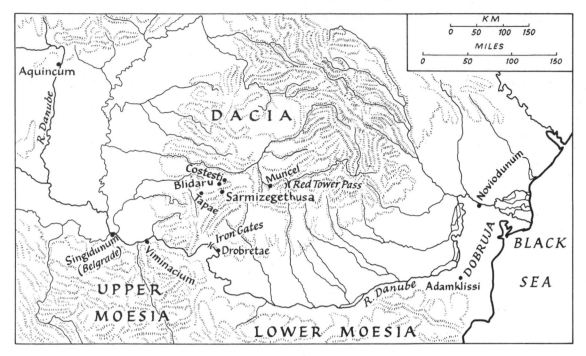

Eastern Europe at the time of Trajan's conquest of Dacia.

archaeology is of some help. On the plateau of Adamklissi in the area of modern Romania known as the Dobruja, not far from the mouth of the Danube, stand three remarkable Roman monuments. One of them will be mentioned again later (page 69): of the other two, one is a mausoleum, 125 feet (38 metres) in diameter, the other is an altar about forty feet (twelve metres) square, covered with the names of Roman troops who died in action. There can be little doubt that these two structures, sited at either end of an extensive parade ground, represent the site where the army gathered annually to offer sacrifice to the gods for the souls of their dead comrades. Whether or not it is the actual site where the men fell we will never know. Some scholars have argued that it was here that the governor of Moesia was killed in 85, others that it was the site of the defeat of Fuscus two years later. At any event it must have been a particularly solemn spot where the tragic defeats which initiated the wars with the Dacians were remembered with bitterness—until, that is, a great victory should expiate the memory.

Some measure of Roman retribution came a year or so later in 89 at the battle of Tapae; the Dacians were thoroughly routed and their leader Decebalus was forced to negotiate a peace settlement. Actually the peace terms were extremely favourable to Decebalus; he had to pay an annual sum of money to Rome and allow the

Roman armies to pass through his territory, but in return he was recognised as king of Dacia by the Emperor and received a number of Roman engineers to help him with construction work. That the Emperor did not regard the victory as significant is shown by the fact that he declined to take the title of 'Dacicus' after the settlement. Had the campaign been thought to be successful, he would surely have done so.

For the next ten years or so an uneasy peace was maintained with the Dacians, although the Romans faced almost constant threats from their western Germanic neighbours. By 98, however, the year in which Trajan came to power, the situation along the lower Danube was beginning to look serious again; there were rumours that Decebalus was strengthening his strongholds in readiness for an attack. Trajan decided to take the initiative and by the spring of 101 he was ready to launch his invasion.

We know relatively little of Trajan's adversary Decebalus. He came to power in the year 86, when the old Dacian king Duras Diurpaneus abdicated, and in the next year was powerful enough to annihilate the Roman army near Adamklissi. For twenty years, until his death in 106, he led his people with perseverance and courage. From the reliefs which depict him, he seems to have been a tall man, bearded, with long hair, a long straight nose and heavy eyebrows, features which Trajan's forces would have got to know when the king's severed head was paraded among them in the last days of the war.

The kingdom which Decebalus ruled was developing rapidly. By the time it came into conflict with Rome the Dacian state was fast becoming an urban civilisation in its own right. We hear a little about the Dacians from classical writers in the second century BC. By the beginning of the first century BC it seems that their power was concentrating in the Transylvanian mountains, where one of the powerful chieftains, Burebista, had succeeded in setting himself up as leader of most of the individual Dacian tribes. The geographer Strabo claims that Burebista's force amounted to 200,000 warriors with whom he advanced westwards, conquering the Celtic tribes in his way until he reached central Czechoslovakia. A few years later he expanded eastwards to engulf the rich lands and cities around the western shores of the Black Sea. By 48 BC he was strong enough to intervene in the Roman power struggle and offer Pompey support against Caesar. The offer came too late, but it demonstrates something of the power of the Dacian state. The king was assassinated in the late 40s and thereafter, in the internal conflict which followed, the core of the state was divided between a number of local kings, while the outlying territories were lost. But as Rome advanced the various factions came together once more for their own protection. It was this kingdom to which Decebalus succeeded in AD 86 at a time when the Dacians and the Romans were locked together in mortal conflict.

Dacia was admirably suited to absorb many aspects of advanced technology from both the Greeks and the Romans, who were their close neighbours in the south, while from the east and south the brilliance of Thracian and Scythian art served as a constant inspiration to Dacian craftsmen. By the time of the Trajanic wars, Dacian civilisation had reached a peak: great *oppida* like Sarmizegethusa had now become towns in their own right, sites of centralised power, government and commerce defended by a network of minor *oppida* and outposts. Trade and production were well organised; the most important resource was silver which was exploited to make coins to facilitate internal and external trade, and to make superb works of craftsmanship—drinking vessels, personal ornaments, and so on which were so much in demand by the upper-class patrons. The workshops of silversmiths have been found in several Dacian *oppida*. Iron was extremely important and was extensively employed in construction works: it was also widely used to make tools and weapons of every conceivable kind, even such specialised items as crampons, to facilitate walking on ice and snow. Specialist potters were to be found in practically every major settlement, making an elegant range of dishes, plates and bowls for a market that was obviously used to products of quality.

The high level of craftsmanship evidently depended for its continued inspiration on extensive trade with the Romanised world to the south. In return for Dacian products such as silver, furs and probably slaves, the Roman traders offered oil, wine and other luxury goods as well as direct payment in cash. Vast numbers of Roman silver *denarii* were in common use in Dacia, completely replacing old-established local coinages.

In parallel with this political and economic development came advances in religious and cultural life. There is now clear evidence to show that the Dacians could write using Greek and Latin script. In a sacred precinct in their capital at Sarmizegethusa, blocks were found inscribed with the names of priests in Greek characters, and a pottery vessel stamped with the name of Decebalus in Latin script has been found. There is also some hint in the classical sources that

Silver harness
decoration from Dacia,
first century BC.

Dacian astronomy had reached a high level of achievement—a fact borne out by the discovery of a circular sanctuary in Sarmizegethusa divided into three precincts with stone pillars representing days, a circle of wooden pillars for seasons and a horse-shoe setting of timbers for the years. The year was divided into twelve months each of thirty days, the equivalent to the week being six days.

The Dacia which Trajan was to subdue was therefore no crude backland of barbarian savages. It had learnt much from its neighbours—alphabets, craft skills and principles of architecture—but it had moulded them together in a distinctive way so that one can fairly speak of the emergence of a Dacian civilisation. Just as the pace of creative life was gaining momentum, however, Trajan struck.

The Roman army had been assembled at Viminacium, a military base on the south bank of the Danube. Trajan's Column shows the army crossing the river on two pontoon bridges, either (as some people suggest) to facilitate a single crossing, or to represent two separate crossings at different places, after which the forces would have met for the march on Sarmizegethusa. They seem to have got as far as Tapae, the scene of the earlier Roman victory, before they met any serious opposition, but there they were confronted by a substantial native force. The indecisive battle which ensued was fought in a thunderstorm which the sculptors of the Column have indicated with a representation of the god Jupiter, naturally enough taking the Roman side and hurling thunderbolts at the bedraggled Dacians. What followed is difficult to untangle, but it seems probable that after trying to negotiate, Decebalus resorted to a scorched earth policy and retreated further into the mountains, killing off livestock and burning crops so as to hinder the Romans. After a further period of advance Trajan wisely decided to withdraw his troops to winter quarters. Decebalus evidently wished to press home his advantage and during the winter organised with his eastern neighbours, the Roxolani, a concerted attack on the Romans. It seems that the province of Lower Moesia received the brunt of the raid, but Trajan's troops were able to cope and drove the raiders back.

During the winter the army busied themselves with preparations for the next year's campaign. It is wrong to think of them as simply a fighting force. They were far more than that—above all they were excellent engineers and builders. Winter was a time when equipment could be manufactured and repaired, when siege instruments, boats and carts could be built and when engineering work could be

Roman legionaries
constructing a fort
during one of the
campaigns. A relief
from Trajan's
Column in Rome.

undertaken. In newly conquered territory there was much to be done. Only a year before the campaign had begun Trajan had undertaken one of the most fascinating feats of road building on record. He had decided to build a proper road along the south bank of the Danube to link the various forts along the line, and in particular to improve the old-established route between his two major bases at Viminacium and Drobretae. Much of the route was comparatively easy to engineer, but along the length of the Danube now known as the Iron Gates the river flows for miles through a deep gorge with sheer limestone sides, formed where the river cuts through a range of the Carpathian Mountains. For the incredible distance of twelve miles (19·3 kilometres) along the gorge, the army engineers had carved a shelf about six feet (1·83 metres) wide which was increased to twelve feet (3·66 metres) in width by means of a wooden platform cantilevered out over the torrent. The ledge and the socket holes for the timber platform were visible until recently but are now submerged beneath the waters dammed back by a new hydro-electricity scheme. All that will be saved is

Trajan's road along the Danube. The almost vertical face of the gorge was cut back to form a ledge but part of the road was cantilevered out over the water. The ledge still survives together with the holes for the timber framework beneath.

the rock-cut inscription by which the road building project was commemorated by an army sculptor.

It was probably in the winter of 101, while stationed at Drobretae, that the army constructors completed another masterpiece of engineering—a permanent bridge across the Danube. It was designed by Trajan's architect Apollodorus (the architect who was later to take charge of the forum building project in Rome) and was half a mile (0.8 kilometres) long. We know of it from two sources— an enthusiastic description given by the historian Cassius Dio, and a visual representation on Trajan's Column. According to Dio, it stood on twenty stone-built piers, each 150 feet (46 metres) high, sixty feet (18 metres) wide and 170 feet (52 metres) apart. The Column relief shows a somewhat shortened version, but depicts the stone piers and timber work in brilliant detail. On the top of each pier we can see the timber cradling composed of three horizontal

A reconstruction of Trajan's famous bridge across the Danube. It is described in detail by a contemporary writer and also illustrated on Trajan's Column.

OPPOSITE
Silver drinking-horn
from Dacia, early
third century BC.

rows laid at right angles to each other. On these, pairs of braced trestles were placed to support a series of joists carrying the planking of the roadway. The trestles also formed the springers for wooden segmental arches which spanned the spaces between the piers and gave support to the roadway above. To complete the work the roadway was provided with handrails. In spite of Dio's exaggeration and the sculptors' simplification, the two sources of evidence combine to give an unparalleled idea of a masterpiece of military engineering which gained justifiable fame in its day. Never let it be supposed that the army was idle between campaigns.

In the spring of 102 Trajan was ready. This time the plan was to attack Sarmizegethusa from the east through the Red Tower Pass. Again Decebalus sent emissaries, minor nobles at first, whom Trajan refused to see, and finally members of the prominent aristocracy. The terms were unacceptable, and Decebalus refused them. Trajan therefore pressed on, storming en route a fortress at Muncel. After a further battle, Decebalus entered the Roman camp in person to make his submission and offer surrender. The terms were not particularly exacting: the western part of Dacia was given up to the Romans, and the forts dismantled, while all his engines of war were to be handed over. At the same time he had to agree to accept a Roman garrison at Sarmizegethusa. The episode is summed up on the Column by a moving scene in which the displaced Dacian population is seen streaming out of the annexed territory, men, women and children, driving their flocks before them.

In recent years Romanian archaeologists, in particular Professors C. and H. Daicoviciu, have devoted much time to the study of the Dacian forts against which Trajan's army had to fight. One site of outstanding interest is Piatra Rosie, sited on top of a steep hill of red rock, guarding the south-western approach to Sarmizegethusa. On the summit was built a rectangular walled enclosure with massive towers at the corners, in one of which was the main entrance reached by a fine stone-built staircase. Outside the main fort and extending down the slope a larger enclosure had been built of vertical timbers set close together in the earth, forming a continuous fence but with masonry towers at the two lower corners. Here is evidently one of the series of strongpoints which were being erected in the first century AD to form a protective screen around the capital city of Sarmizegethusa.

Piatra Rosie is of particular interest because it is depicted in all

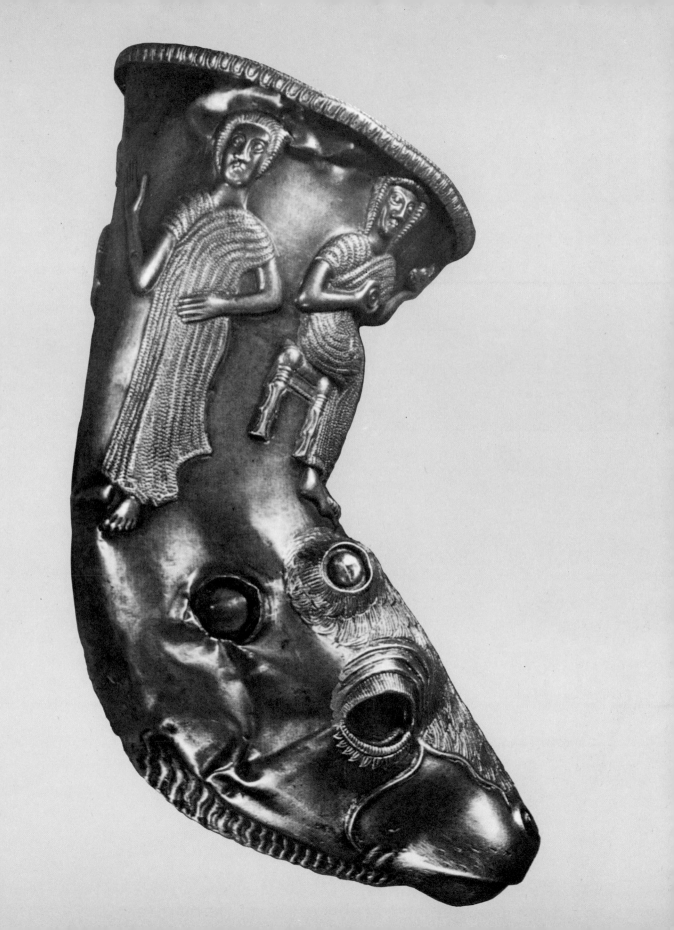

its detail on Trajan's Column. Dacian soldiers are shown cutting down trees to erect a timber palisade on either side of a great stone tower. Then we see the initial Roman attack by auxiliaries under protective fire from a corps of archers. After a struggle the Dacians fall back into the safety of the inner stone fort, but the legionaries, shields locked above their heads in the classic *testudo* (tortoise) manoeuvre, approach the gate up a flight of stone steps. Practically every detail of the fort, as exposed by excavation, has been faithfully recorded by the Roman war artist—there can be very little doubt that he was there in person making his sketches at the moment of the attack.

A number of other Dacian strongholds are shown on the Column, but they cannot with such certainty be related to excavated structures. At the point which in the Column is thought to refer to the beginning of the Second Dacian War, in 105, Decebalus together with a number of other Dacian nobles are shown congregating in a fort built of large blocks of masonry and divided down the centre by a partition wall. A very similar structure has been excavated at Blidaru, guarding the north-western approach to Sarmizegethusa, but positive identification is impossible. Much the same doubt attaches to the recognition of Costești, one of the principal Dacian strongholds. The actual site is well known and has been excavated, showing that a substantial wall enclosed an irregular area of the hilltop within which were stone-built towers commanding the view of the approach for miles around. Although several attempts have been made to identify Costești among the varied representations of Dacian fortifications on the Column, there is still no certainty as to which it is.

The fortifications of the Dacians were very sophisticated structures which incorporated many ideas derived from Greek and Roman architecture, but their weapons were distinctively local. Their oval-shaped shields are illustrated several times on Trajan's Column: they are made of wood or hide, edged and strengthened with metal strips and sometimes lined with iron plates. Nearly always they are shown to be highly decorated, just like the one found at Piatra Rosie which is enlivened with plant motifs and has a representation of a boar in the centre. Weapons commonly in use included arrows, swords and spears as well as two local specialities, the curved dagger called the *sica* and heavier curved sabre (*falces*) both of which were particularly feared by the Roman soldiers: with the sabre you could lop off an opponent's arm with very little

Dacians defending the timber gate of one of their fortresses against Roman attack. Roman soldiers are seen here adopting the 'tortoise' formation. A relief from Trajan's Column in Rome.

difficulty! The Dacian force, fighting on its own ground, protected by its carefully constructed fortifications, must have been a formidable foe. Imagine the horror which the Roman troops must have felt as they approached one fortification only to be faced with a high wall fronted by lily pits of the kind which Caesar dug at Alesia (page 29), while behind the wall, hoisted aloft on poles, was a row of severed heads—no doubt hacked from the bodies of Romans killed in battle. There must have been considerable relief when surrender terms were arranged in 102 and the army could move out of these foreign mountains in triumph.

With all but a small garrison gone, Decebalus was not slow to re-arm. Contrary to the agreement he welcomed Roman deserters, who were of considerable assistance in helping him to refortify according to Roman standards. By 105 he had built up a sufficiently well-armed force to feel able to attack once more. When he was ready he persuaded the commander of the Roman garrison of Sarmizegethusa, Longinus, to visit him, and immediately took him as a hostage. Then messages were sent to the Emperor to demand the return of the annexed territories in the west, as well as cash compensation for the previous war. Trajan was clearly in a difficult position, but the dilemma was solved by Longinus, who took poison and died, thus leaving Trajan free to act. But before a force could be mustered, Decebalus took the initiative and swept down on the province of Moesia. It was all that the Emperor could do to relieve the beleaguered province before the campaigning season of 105 was over.

In 106 all was ready for the advance. The Roman forces were divided into two columns for the initial stages, but they seem to have converged before reaching Sarmizegethusa, to approach as one body for the final kill. The siege of Sarmizegethusa is shown in brilliant detail on the Column. We can see the Roman siege camp with the soldiers' leather tents pitched inside, while nearby the assault is in progress. The town wall is shown as constructed of courses of faced rubble tied together with horizontal rows of timbers, the ends of which projected through the masonry face: at intervals there are tall wooden towers. The defenders huddle inside protecting themselves from the Roman slingers while they hurl rocks and spears at the approaching troops. But already the defences are falling. We see the ladders being brought up to the wall and in one place a Roman soldier has climbed to the top and cut off an enemy's head which he keeps as a trophy. All the energy and horror of the final siege is vividly displayed. At last, when all seemed to be lost, some of the nobles drank poison, others set fire to the buildings, while some, including Decebalus, managed to escape.

The site of Sarmizegethusa itself is well known and has been the scene of extensive excavations. It was no rough barbarian hideout. Within and nearby were buildings of considerable quality—the sanctuaries referred to above, the house of a surgeon in which a set of medical implements was recovered, workshops for ironsmiths and the craftsmen working in silver, as well as private houses of timber and daub on stone foundations. All parts of the town were provided with fresh water from springs in the nearby hills. The water was conveyed to the town in an aqueduct built of tiles, which led into a timber collecting-tank where the sediment was allowed to settle before the cleared water was channelled to the individual houses in baked clay pipes. Life had been comfortable and well ordered, but now at last the peace was shattered, the town ruined and many of its inhabitants lay slaughtered in the ashes.

Those who fled were eagerly pursued and cut down. At last Decebalus himself was surrounded, but rather than be taken captive he committed suicide by slitting his own throat. The scene is dramatically displayed on the Column: we see Decebalus cowering under a tree with his sword already at his neck. As the Roman cavalry moves in, a trooper stretches out his hand in a vain attempt to stop the king killing himself.

By a remarkable chance a discovery made as far away as Philippi in Macedonia adds a little more to the final scene: in 1965 the tomb-stone of a cavalry officer named Tiberius Claudius Maximus was found, and in the long description of his career carved on the stone we are told that he was the captor of King Decebalus. The famous scene is enacted once more in a small panel carved at the head of the stone. Maximus, with sword in his right hand, holding two spears and the reins of his horse in the other, arrives just too late. Decebalus, dressed as a typical Dacian chieftain in trousers, a long cloak and pointed hat, has just sunk to the ground, his shield still on his left arm, while his curved sword falls from his right hand. It is tempting to imagine the old veteran Maximus giving instructions to the man who was to carve his tombstone, telling him precisely how it was on that fateful day when he arrived just too late to take Decebalus alive.

With the war over and the Dacian leadership destroyed, Trajan decided to annex a substantial part of the country as a Roman

TICLAVDIV
MXIMVSVET

The carving on the top of the tombstone of Tiberius Claudius Maximus, the captor of Decebalus, from Philippi in Macedonia.

province. A colony with the title of Ulpia Traiana was founded not far from Sarmizegethusa, other towns grew up, the silver, gold and salt mines were exploited and for over 150 years the province developed in comparative peace, providing many detachments of auxiliary soldiers to fight for Rome in far-flung wars.

The death of Decebalus was not quite the end of the campaign for Trajan. There were mopping-up operations to be carried out in various parts of the country, particularly in the east, culminating in a return to Adamklissi, to the hill of the cenotaph dedicated to the Roman soldiers who had been killed in the devastating defeats of the mid-80s. Here in 108 Trajan erected a vast circular monument a hundred feet (thirty metres) in diameter capped by a hexagonal pedestal supporting a representation of a lopped tree spread about with the spoils of war. This was a symbolic representation in stone of the *tropaeum* (trophy) often erected at the end of a victorious

69

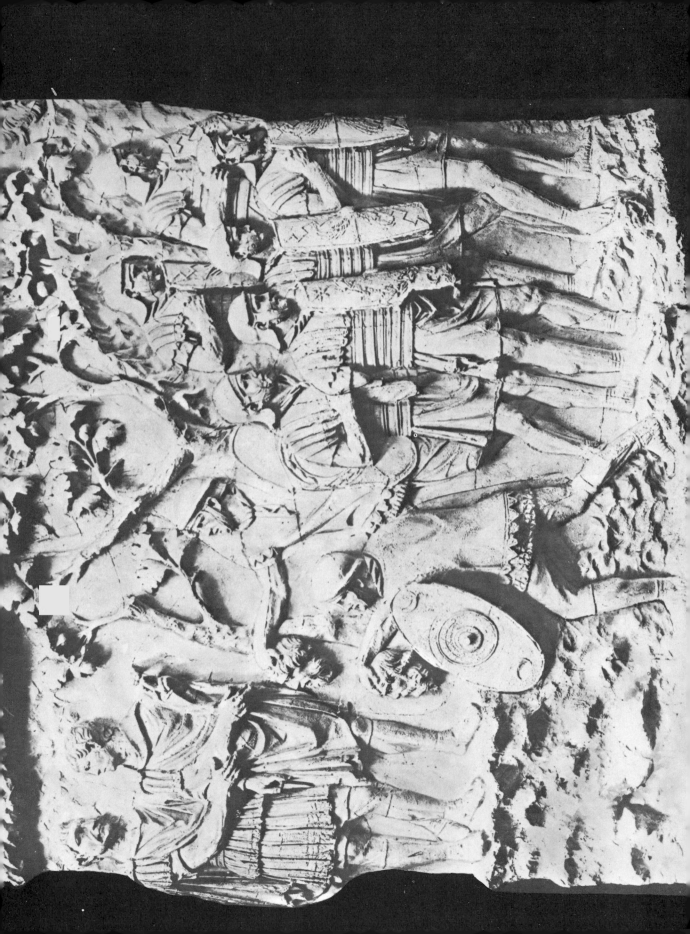

Roman soldiers present Trajan with the heads of two of the enemy during one of his Dacian campaigns. A relief from Trajan's Column in Rome.

battle. Below the tree were statues of four barbarians, sitting or standing in chains. The circular wall which surrounded the base of the monument was decorated with two series of sculptures, the upper panels depicting chained barbarians identifiable from their dress as Germans, Dacians and Sarmatians, the enemies who had been overcome, while the lower series illustrates episodes from the campaigns. Here then was a monument to the completion of the Dacian war—a monument to great Roman victories, situated close to the altar and mausoleum which commemorated Rome's earlier defeats. The score had now been settled: significantly the trophy is dedicated to *Mars Ultor*—Mars the Avenger.

5

Frontier Towns

At the time when barbarian Europe was overrun by the Roman army, native communities were already fast developing as urban states. Admittedly, the towns which grew up under Roman rule were more ordered in their layout, often conforming to a series of preconceived designs, and more elaborate in their appearance, adorned with fine monumental buildings, but many of the functions which they carried out were the same as those of their native predecessors. Above all, they served as centres where the products of the region could be redistributed and where raw materials could be converted into consumer goods—in other words, centres for trade and industry. In addition they were places where the traditions and rules of the society were established and periodically restated in meetings both religious and secular. This would require a religious focus such as a temple or shrine, and provision for tribal assemblies.

The impact of Roman rule did not greatly alter the structure of these barbarian societies, it simply formalised it and imposed additional rules and restraints which gave rise to a remarkable degree of conformity across the face of the entire Roman provincial world— the organisation of local government at Gorsium, a town in the heart of Hungary, would have been entirely familiar to a native of Caerwent on the south Welsh coastal plain.

We have already seen something of the urban situation among the Dacians in the first century AD, but that was a situation which undoubtedly owed much to influence from the Roman and Greek world, and was therefore perhaps a rather special case. So we must begin this brief survey of frontier towns by looking at a native capital (*oppidum*) where Roman influence was at a minimum. The choice naturally falls on Manching, near Ingolstadt, in southern Germany.

Manching lies on a terrace overlooking the Danube in the territory of the Vindelici, a powerful tribe who once occupied the land between the north flank of the Alps and the River Danube. The Vindelici maintained their independence until 15 BC when they succumbed to the Roman armies led by Tiberius and Drusus who were at this time engaged on campaigns of conquest in the Alps. Manching is magnificently situated to control two major trade-routes, the one along the Danube from east to west, and the other crossing the river at this point and joining the Roman world of the south to the north European plain. It had flourished for fifty to a hundred years before the Roman conquest.

Although the site had been known for some time, it was not until 1936, when a military airfield was being constructed, that any serious archaeological work was undertaken. But the area of the *oppidum* was so large that relatively little could be done. In fact the defended enclosure was about nine hundred acres in extent and the bank and ditch which enclosed it on three sides (the fourth being the marshy valley of a stream) ran for nearly four and a half miles (7·2 kilometres)! Faced with this enormous site all the excavator could do was to examine the structure of the defences. These he showed to have been constructed in the manner which Caesar described as typical of Gaulish defences he called *murus Gallicus* (Gallic walls). The method was to build an outer stone face and link it by horizontal timbers to a grid of timbers laid at right angles to each other, nailed together layer upon layer. The resulting box-like structure was then filled with stone rubble. It gave an extremely resilient defence, capable of rendering the Roman battering rams almost completely useless. Such a defence had been provided at Manching in the first period of its occupation, but at a later stage when the wall had become dilapidated it was refaced using vertical timbers and dry-stone walling.

During the Second World War the Manching airfield suffered extensive bomb damage, but in 1955 it was decided to make it operational again. The excavators, now led by Professor Krämer, the director of the Römisch-Germanische Kommission, were faced with the problem of how to tackle this vast site of nine hundred acres. It was first necessary to find out if the site had been occupied and if so where the occupation was at its densest. This Krämer did by using a digging machine to cut five miles (eight kilometres) of trial

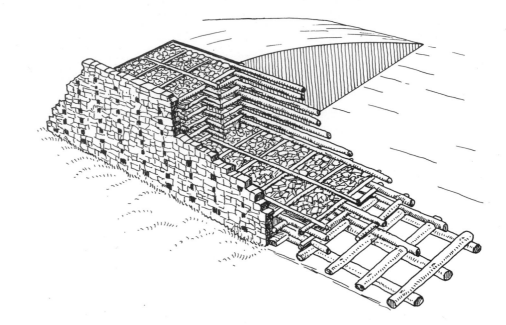

A reconstruction of the defences of the Celtic fortress of Manching. Caesar referred to this type of wall as a *murus Gallicus*.

trenches, from which he was able to tell that apart from a clear band of a few hundred yards or so inside the ramparts, the interior had been densely occupied. Having established this, there was nothing for it but to begin the total and systematic stripping of vast areas. Gradually the plan of houses and streets began to emerge and from the enormous quantities of pottery, small objects and animal bones, a picture of the life of the *oppidum* could begin to be built up.

Farming clearly provided the subsistence basis of the community. Over a quarter of a million animal bones were recovered, showing that pigs were the most numerous, with cattle and sheep coming second and third. Dogs and horses were also represented, but in smaller numbers.

Manching also seems to have been an important centre for production. High-quality pottery was manufactured, iron ore was dug out of nearby bogs and smelted outside the town (the iron ingots being worked in smithies inside), and there was ample evidence for the production of various objects in copper and bronze. Other specialist trades probably included the manufacture of glass beads and bracelets, the evidence coming from the discovery of large lumps of raw purple glass. The importance of Manching as a trading centre is further emphasised by the discovery of pieces of clay moulds in which the blanks for gold coins were made. These blanks would then have been struck between two dies to form the actual coin. One of the moulds actually contained droplets of gold

74

alloy of the same composition as the local Vindelican gold coins found on the site. Long-distance trade was also practised. The excavators found fragments of Italian amphorae which had been used to convey wine to the barbarian north, together with fine imported pottery, and bronze and glass tableware.

From this great wealth of material a picture can be built up of a vigorous town growing rich on trade and production, and supporting a resident population, many of them specialists, probably running into many thousands. The end came probably in 15 BC: all that was left in the wake of a violent attack was a deserted site scattered with the broken and buckled weapons of its defenders.

Oppida of the type so clearly displayed by the excavations at Manching are to be found in most parts of Celtic Europe. They represent the culmination of urban development in the period immediately preceding the Roman invasion. Sometimes, as at Manching, the invasion put an end to the life of the site, but elsewhere, for example at Alesia and Gergovia, the scenes of two of Caesar's bitterest battles, the towns continued to develop under Roman rule. Each example was different, depending upon the local conditions and the needs of the Roman military government.

A particularly interesting example is provided by the remains found at Budapest, capital of Hungary, once the site of the Roman settlement of Aquincum, one of the foremost cities in the province of Pannonia. The modern city of Budapest is really two separate towns, Buda on the west side of the Danube and Pest on the east, unified as one city in 1873. The Buda side of the river is dominated by a great limestone hill known as Gellérthegy (Gellért hill) which was chosen by the local Celtic tribe, the Eraviscans, as their principal *oppidum*. It seems likely that the hill was more of a stronghold while the main occupied area straggled, apparently undefended, at the foot of the hill in the area now called Tabán. This particular Celtic group had every need for a strongly fortified place of refuge, since they were at different times under pressure from the Germanic Cimbri as well as the Dacians, who were then spreading westwards under Burebista. Although excavation on the Gellért-Tabán settlement has been restricted, sufficient has been recovered to show that it was very much a town in the tradition of Manching, complete with a mint and artisan quarters where pottery was being manufactured.

The Roman armies moved into this part of the Danube basin

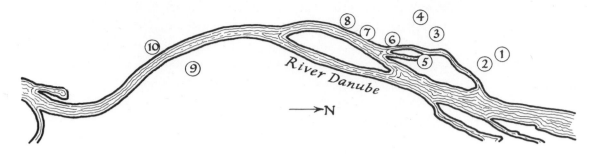

Roman sites along the Danube now within the boundaries of modern Budapest.

1 Ruins of civil amphitheatre
2 Ruins of civil town
3 Villa
4 Christian sepulchral chapel
5 Palace of the Emperor's proconsuls
6 Military bath
7 Museum of the military town
8 Military amphitheatre
9 Contra-Aquincum
10 Gellérthegy (native settlement)

some time after 10 BC, but their hold on the area was, to start with, somewhat tenuous. While there were three legions in the province of Pannonia by AD 14 they were all stationed in the south-west, not far from the Italian border. By the second half of the first century AD the Danube bank itself seems to have been protected by auxiliary detachments, one of which was based at Aquincum several miles up river from the native *oppidum*. What relationship existed between the two is difficult to define on the present evidence, but it is not improbable that the natives continued to occupy their old city although some of them, traders of various kinds, may well have moved up stream to camp near the military base to provide goods and services for the troops.

Towards the end of the first century AD, as the result of increasing troubles with the Dacians, the Emperor Domitian decided to move a legion up to the site of Aquincum, which naturally meant the complete rebuilding of the base to provide suitable accommodation for the enlarged force. By the beginning of the second century the native population living outside the walls of the fortress had greatly increased, to such an extent that the old *oppidum* must by now have been totally abandoned. There were of course great attractions to living close to the fortress: the road connections were

76

better and the 6,000 or so troops provided ready customers for the traders who set up shop in the camp town (*canabae*). Moreover, although the soldiers were, at this period, forbidden to marry, they were permitted to house their unofficial wives and children nearby.

It would be quite wrong to think of the *canabae* as a squalid and ramshackle shanty town. Far from it; it seems to have been well laid out with regular streets, a water supply tapped from the military aqueduct, a masonry-built market centre or forum, and a number of quite luxurious houses, some of them with painted walls and mosaic floors. Its population, though basically Eraviscan, would have been swollen by traders and merchants of other nationalities and retired soldiers who once had served in the province. In this way the native Celts absorbed and became absorbed in the Roman way of life.

The legionary fortress and its *canabae* now lie in the area of Budapest known as Obuda (Old Buda), a once elegant suburb now being rapidly redeveloped to provide flats for the growing population of the city. As the old buildings are demolished so new blocks of flats spring up to replace them, leaving very little time for the team of archaeologists to carry out their rescue excavations. The situation is the same in practically every great historical city in Europe—too little time and money for the archaeologists to complete their work adequately before the buried remains are destroyed, or obscured beneath tons of modern concrete. But in spite of all these difficulties, a small team of Hungarian archaeologists led by Dr Klára Póczy are at this moment recovering a great deal of informa-

A reconstruction of a typical private house in Aquincum.

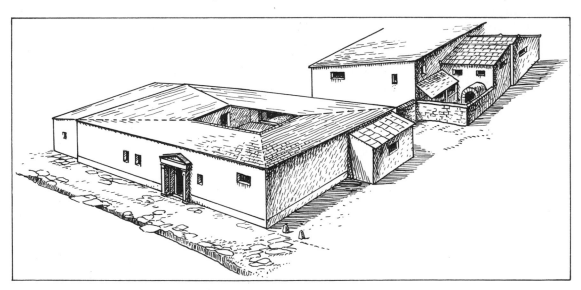

One of the forward-projecting bastions on the wall of the bridge-head fort on the Pest side of the river. The fort guards the point at which the ferry crossed the Danube at Contra Aquincum. *See page 80.*

tion about the fortress. For the first time the lines of its defensive walls have been defined and the stone interval towers arranged along it are being examined, providing evidence of the various rebuildings to which the fortress was subjected during its long life. Unfortunately most of the sites will have to be refilled to allow building developments to be completed, but in the case of exceptional buildings such as the military bathing establishment and one of the main gates of the fortress, the modern buildings have been modified to allow the Roman structures to be preserved and left open to the public. Driving out from the centre of Budapest, the first sign the visitor now sees to remind him that he is approaching the fortress is the huge military amphitheatre built in the second century, where games and military exercises would have been carried out. The fact that it had a capacity for 10,000 gives some idea of the size of the community.

One of the results of the Dacian wars was that Trajan decided to split the province of Pannonia into two parts to ease administrative difficulties. As a result of this Aquincum became the capital of Lower Pannonia, which greatly increased the prestige and status of the town. To fit it for its new position a splendid palace was built on the island of Hajógyár in the Danube, just opposite the fortress. It was evidently a most elaborate and commanding structure dominated by a monumental façade overlooking the river. Here the legate of the Emperor would have lived in state and entertained his guests on the very fringe of the Roman world, looking across the narrow stretch of water towards the lands beyond the Empire. The first legate to occupy the palace later became the Emperor Hadrian.

About one and a quarter miles (1·7 kilometres) up river from the fortress and *canabae* lies a second large urban complex—the civilian town of Aquincum, discovered and excavated towards the end of the nineteenth century and in recent years consolidated and partially reconstructed. By the beginning of the second century the civilian town had become important and it was the Emperor Hadrian, who no doubt knew it well from his stay in the area, who conferred on the community the rank of *municipium*. Municipal rank gave the citizens certain legal rights which were very advantageous at the time. Seventy years later the Emperor Septimius Severus upgraded the community yet again, giving it the title of a *colonia*. Variations in status between the inhabitants of towns of different ranks were eventually swept away by Caracalla in 214, who extended the full rights of Roman citizenship to all free-born provincials.

The part of the civilian town now exposed to visitors gives a very full idea of what a prosperous urban community looked like. There are regularly laid-out streets, some of them lined by shops, and a wide range of public buildings, including a market place (*forum*) and law courts (*basilica*), a suite of public baths, a specialised market hall (*macellum*), several shrines (including one to the Eastern god Mithras), the headquarters of a youth guild, and of course a number of private houses, some of them adorned with mosaic pavements and painted walls. The city was also provided with a fresh water supply by means of an aqueduct, and for the amusement of its citizens a substantial civilian amphitheatre had been built just outside the city wall. Even though the civilian town of Aquincum lay on the very edge of the Empire, it showed all the luxuries and comforts which a town anywhere in the Roman Empire might have expected.

Aquincum owed much of its prosperity to its position on the frontier. It was admirably sited to engage in trade with the barbarian world. Vast quantities of Roman luxury objects—elaborate table-

ware in bronze, silver and glass, coins, wine and a host of other
desirable goods—would have been traded to the barbarians in return
for things that the Roman world most prized, such as wild animals
for the arenas of Rome, furs and slaves. There were distinct advantages to being on the edge of the Empire; but there were also dis-
advantages, as the citizens were soon to find. Between 167 and 180 a
new and violent war broke out on their very doorstep—the war
with the Marcomanni. Between 167 and 171 these Germanic peoples
ravaged the Roman province, burning both settlements at Aquincum. By 171, though the Emperor Marcus Aurelius had managed
to force the war back on the enemy territory, he was now committed
to engage in a series of exhausting campaigns against the Marcomanni, the Quadi and the Iazyges. By 175 the situation seemed
secure, but two years later fighting broke out again, and it was not
until 180 that a lasting peace settlement was concluded. Although
the terms were favourable to Rome, requiring among other things
that the barbarian territory fronting the Danube be vacated, and that
its inhabitants should not be allowed to use their own ships on the
Danube or land on any of the islands, the war was a frightening
reminder to the inhabitants of Aquincum of just how vulnerable
they really were. The memory of the disaster must have been ever
present.

A further raid by the Germans, some time about 260, marked the
beginning of the end. The barbarian threat was never to be far away
now. A generation later, in 294, the Emperor Diocletian, who was
responsible for so much military reorganisation along the frontiers,
visited Aquincum to inspect the building of a new bridgehead
fortification. Part of the wall with some massive projecting bastions
was first identified in 1779, and can still be seen on the Pest side of
the river close to the point at which the Elizabeth Bridge now crosses
the Danube. The function of the fortlet was quite simply to protect
the ferry-terminal which linked the Roman province to the barbarian
world. Visiting the well-displayed ruins now, in the heart of modern
Budapest, it is difficult to imagine the loneliness and fear which
must have been constantly in the minds of the little garrison as they
stared out at the enemy across the great Hungarian plain, alert to
every movement.

The end came rapidly after 374, when the Emperor Valentinian
ordered further refortifications to the walls of Aquincum. In 1973
one of the gates probably belonging to this period was uncovered
by the rescue archaeologists working on a building site in Obuda.

Above Gorsium: the
front wall façade of
the provincial temple
with the partially
reconstructed
nymphaeum (orna-
mental fountain)
on the left.
Below The tombstone
of a Pannonian
matron, Flavia Usaiu,
from Gorsium.

By 378 most of the population had abandoned the civil town to crowd within the walls of the fortress, but by 409 the pressure from the barbarians had become so great that those remaining moved away from the frontier to seek protection further inland.

The early history of Aquincum, the move from Gellérthegy to the fortress, the growth of the civilian town, the regression and the final abandonment, is typical of so many frontier towns in all parts of the Roman Empire. The vividness of much of the detail is a tribute to the efforts of the teams of Hungarian archaeologists who, for the last two hundred years, have laboured, and still are labouring, to rescue and piece together the fragments of the jigsaw.

About fifty miles (eighty kilometres) south-west of Aquincum, in the gentle rolling countryside of Transdanabia, lies the little village of Tác, not far from the town of Székesfehérvár. For years Roman remains have been known from the neighbourhood, but it was not until serious work began in 1958, under the direction of Dr Jeno Fitz, that the full importance of the site began to be realised. Previous investigators believed that the site was a Roman villa but Dr Fitz has been able to show that here lay the Roman town of Gorsium, probably the largest in the province of Lower Pannonia. Although only a comparatively small portion of its area has yet been excavated, parts of the story are already becoming clear.

It seems that Gorsium began its life as a fort for an auxiliary cavalry unit, the *ala I Scubulorum*, which in the middle of the first century AD was billeted here to guard an important crossroads. The site of another fort is recorded in the neighbourhood, but its exact construction date is unknown. The precise identification of the detachment is known because fortunately they made their own bricks and stamped them with the name of their unit. The fort remained in use for several years, and as might be expected the local inhabitants were gradually attracted to it, setting up a small village (*vicus*) of simple timber huts with sunken floors just outside the defences, exactly as had happened at Aquincum. These huts were of purely native type so there is no doubt that the *vicus* was occupied by the local Celtic Eraviscans.

It was during the reign of Trajan that the first major alterations took place. The fort was levelled and in its place a series of masonry buildings was erected to form the grand civic centre of what must have been from this time onwards an extremely important town. Before looking at the buildings themselves, we must ask what the official status of Gorsium was. A hint is provided by the tombstone of P. Aelius Respectus, who died towards the end of the second century. Its inscription records that he was *decurio municipii*, which means a town councillor of the *municipium*. Since the *municipium* referred to can only have been Gorsium, it is reasonable to infer that the place, like the civil town of Aquincum, was probably upgraded to the status of *municipium* by Hadrian when he visited Pannonia in 124. This must mean an extremely rapid change in the fortunes of Gorsium. How was it that a relatively modest *vicus* of the late first century could rise to the status of *municipium* in the space of less than thirty years? Something dramatic must have happened in about 106 or 107 when the public buildings were erected.

To understand this we must turn first to a group of three inscriptions found in the neighbourhood. Over the years scholars have argued as to how they should be interpreted, but Dr Fitz has recently made out a convincing case that they all refer in different ways to the provincial shrine of the Imperial cult—concerned with the worship of the Emperor's family. One of them mentions a gathering of priests for an important festival; the second refers to the imperial procession led by the Emperor Septimius Severus in 202 to inaugurate the temple reconstructed by the Emperors; while the third is an altar which once stood in the temple of the 'Deified Marcus'—the Emperor Marcus Aurelius. Although these inscriptions were found, re-used, in neighbouring towns, there can be very little doubt that they originally came from Gorsium, from which we must conclude that the town was important enough to have housed the centre of the shrine of the Imperial cult, and that was here that the provincial council of Lower Pannonia probably met.

Now if we turn to the buildings which Dr Fitz has excavated in the centre of the town, we find that they are in complete harmony with the interpretation based on the inscriptions. Opposite the forum, was a great monumental building which can be interpreted as the *area sacra* (sacred area) composed of two elements, the temple of the Emperor itself and the assembly halls for the annual provincial council meetings. The temple is represented by a huge hall ending in an apsidal recess in which the altar stood, with a separate sanctuary opening from the east wall. At a point central to both, the excavators found a sacrificial pit (*mundus*) which would have been used in the ceremonial inauguration of the building. One half of the pit was divided into five compartments which would have represented the five districts into which the province was divided. To the east of the temple were the five separate halls for the district

OPPOSITE
Plan of a palatial building on the main street of Gorsium. It may have been an official residence. *See page 84.*

82

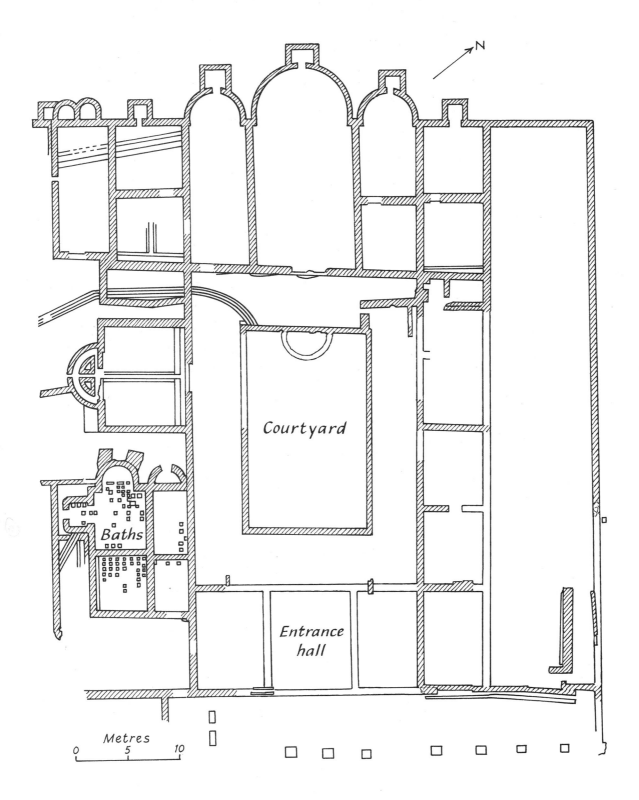

Courtyard

Baths

Entrance
hall

N

Metres
0   5   10

assemblies to meet, opening into a common cross-hall with a recess for the altar to the deified Emperor. The entire complex was fronted by a grand colonnade of granite columns, reached by two flights of steps from the street level and further enlivened by two ornamental fountains. One further detail clinches the identification of this remarkable building: a large number of the bricks used in the construction work were stamped TE-PR—*te*(*mplum*) *pr*(*ovinciae*): the temple of the province.

The second monumental building discovered at Gorsium was a little way down the street from the *area sacra*. It consisted of four suites of rooms arranged around a colonnaded courtyard. The three principal rooms, each with large apses, lay opposite the main entrance hall: on one side was the bath suite, on the other a range of domestic rooms. Such a fine building occupying a central position in the town can hardly be other than a palace, perhaps for the use of the provincial governor and other dignitaries during the annual ceremonies.

Gorsium, then, provides a vivid example of the way in which careful excavations under modern conditions, combined with a meticulous examination of the relevant inscriptions, can revolutionise our understanding of a site: only twenty years ago Gorsium was believed to be just another villa; now it takes its place as one of the primary towns in the province, deliberately chosen to serve as the centre of Imperial worship and the annual meeting place of the provincial council, on the occasion when Trajan divided the province of Pannonia into two parts in 106–7.

Reconstruction of what happened between the middle of the first century and the building programme of 106–7 is difficult. The cavalry unit, *ala I Scubulorum*, occupied the site from the late 40s until some time between 69 and 74, when it was moved to Germany, and probably replaced at Gorsium by the *cohors I Alpinorum*, whose fort has been recognised by aerial photography to the south of the cavalry fort. They remained until the 90s. Throughout this period the civilian *vicus* grew as more natives congregated in the area. We get some idea of the civilian population from their tombstones. One lady, Flavia Usaiu, was a typical Eraviscan female. She is shown wearing a high turban-like bonnet covered with a veil, and adorned with her native-style jewellery—winged brooches on her shoulders, a torque around her neck and heavy bracelets on her wrists. She also carries a staff and a mirror—a formidable matron, no doubt a member of the native aristocracy, who died at the age of eighty some time soon after AD 100. Everything about her dress speaks of her native Celtic origin. Some years later, after the town had grown in status, P. Aelius Respectus died. He was, as we have seen, a decurion, that is, one of the hundred men constituting the town council (*ordo*). Although his gravestone is far more sophisticated, as would befit a dignitary, a scene carved on the bottom of the stone shows two females still dressed in native fashion. The extent of the predominantly native population is even more strongly emphasised by the long list of native names found among the inscriptions from the town. Even so, as the city developed, a number of foreigners moved in to swell the community, mostly, it would seem, from northern Italy although at least one native of North Africa is recorded. These strong links with Italy must to some extent reflect the easy trade connections by road between the two areas.

While the city continued to flourish it was not immune from the barbarian invasions which have been mentioned in connection with Aquincum. After the Marcomannic invasions, during which a number of the buildings were partially destroyed, reconstruction was undertaken on much the same lines, but there were some changes. At the palace, for example, the east wing was dispensed with and a massive granary constructed instead (see page 83).

The wars of 260 caused far more extensive damage: all the principal buildings of the city were irreparably destroyed and rebuilding did not begin until the reign of Diocletian (284–313). Even then no attempt was made to reconstruct the *area sacra*— at least on its original site. Nevertheless the city continued to flourish and no less than two Christian churches were built, a sure indication of its continuing status. A study of the cemetery site suggests that during the fourth century the population increased, possibly as the result of people from the countryside moving into the comparative safety of the town. Details of civic arrangements of the late period have not yet been worked out, but one interesting fact emerges: whereas buildings in the suburbs were abandoned, the city centre showed a great upsurge in activity represented by the discovery of unusually large numbers of coins. The most likely explanation for this is that under Valentinian (364–375) Gorsium, like many of the other towns in the area, was defended by a new city wall designed to protect the central buildings, and the population gradually migrated into the safety of this defended area, leaving outlying buildings deserted: no wall, however, has yet been found.

As a road junction, Gorsium continued to be important well into the Middle Ages; indeed the excavations have produced evidence of practically continuous occupation from the Roman period until the fourteenth century; but as a city it declined rapidly in the fifth century, with the onset of the migration period. The medieval city of the region developed some miles away at Székesfehérvár. This fortunate shift ensured that the ruins of the Roman city remained tolerably intact until 1958, when the present series of excavations began to reveal their true nature.

The last of the three Pannonian towns to be considered is Sopron, the Roman town of Scarbantia, which now lies in the extreme north-west corner of Hungary close to the Austrian border. Sopron owed its importance to the fact that it lay astride the amber route— a very ancient route along which this much prized material, a fossil resin collected on the Baltic coast, was transported south to the Mediterranean world. Trade flourished in the prehistoric period and was still an important part of the economy in the post-Roman era when the Great Moravian Empire (a powerful ninth-century kingdom in Czechoslovakia) emerged to dominate the supply lines along the River Morava.

At the time when the Roman frontier followed the line of the Danube, the focus for the amber trade was the city of Carnuntum. The Roman author Pliny gives a splendid account of how during the reign of Nero a Roman trader called Julianus travelled north through barbarian territories to the Baltic coast, where he visited the local agents and bought from them a great quantity of amber, eventually returning via East Prussia and Poland. How general such journeys were, or became, we do not know, but in all probability much of the collection and transport remained in the hands of the natives who would make their way south along well-tried routes until they reached the frontier at Carnuntum. There the raw material would pass into the hands of Roman middlemen, ready for the next stage of its journey through the provinces of Pannonia and Noricum to the port of Aquileia on the Adriatic coast. From here, on the last stage of its journey, it would be transhipped to the great consumer markets of Italy. The same route in reverse was used to supply the Roman-made commodities, such as bronzeware and glass, used in exchange.

The road between Carnuntum and Aquileia must have been thronged with traders transporting goods between the major towns, Emona, Poetovio, Arrabo, Savaria and Scarbantia (Sopron). Tombstones and inscriptions show us that a particularly high proportion of

Some of the trade routes by which Roman luxury goods were transported into barbarian Europe beyond the frontier.

North Italians, presumably merchants, had settled along the route. Foremost among these were members of the family of Barbii—an influential group of merchants based on Aquileia, whose names crop up at Emona, Savaria, Scarbantia and Carnuntum.

Scarbantia must, then, have been a bustling trading centre. But archaeological discoveries over the years have shown that it was more than just a stopping-off place along the route. It seems that it supported teams of craftsmen able to carve the amber into extremely fine works of art. Savaria, too, yielded similar evidence. Thus, the raw amber which was fed into the system at

Carved ornament of North European amber. It is typical of objects found along the Danube frontier and in the towns along the amber route.

Carnuntum arrived at Aquileia in a form fit to grace any aristocratic Roman household.

Sopron has been the scene of a number of recent excavations, but none is more evocative than that of the north gate of the city, now exposed below ground beneath a medieval tower. It is still possible for the visitor to walk for a short distance along the road—the actual amber route leading up to the gate—and to be reminded of the skill of the local craftsmen by a display of the most exquisite amber carvings found in the various excavations.

6

Gods of the Waters

Of the many hundreds of different deities worshipped all over the Roman world, a surprising number were associated with water. After all, the source of a great river, or a spring (particularly if the water is hot), is always likely to have a certain mystery about it. It was in places like these, in bogs, and in the mature courses of the rivers themselves, that many of the gods were thought to exist, and gods had to be placated with offerings. Most of the important rivers of Europe received dedications from primitive peoples. Weapons and armour, much of it of exquisite quality, were consigned to the waters in enormous quantities. A glance through the British Iron Age galleries of the British Museum will emphasise the point: the finest pieces of parade armour from pre-Roman Britain came from the Thames—the Waterloo Bridge helmet, the Battersea shield, and the shield bosses from Wandsworth—and these are only the more impressive pieces belonging to a much larger collection of finds dredged from the river from time to time during the last 150 years. Some may admittedly have been lost by accident, whilst crossing, but the presence of so much fine material must imply deliberate acts of deposition.

Some indications of the practices involved are provided by what the classical writers say of the Germanic peoples called the Cimbri and Teutones who are believed to have come from Denmark. For fourteen years from 115–101 BC they terrorised barbarian Europe and seriously worried the Roman state, moving from place to place with the utmost ferocity; first in central Europe, then in Gaul, next in Spain, they raided and plundered indiscriminately until in two great battles at Aix-en-Provence in 102 BC and Vercellae in

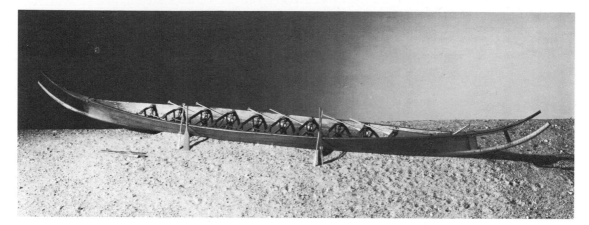

A reconstruction of the Hjortspring boat.

northern Italy in 101, first the Teutones and then the Cimbri were soundly beaten by the Roman general Marius. The warriors were typically Nordic, tall, fair in colouring, and blue-eyed. They were also well used to the rigours and hardships of life. It is said that when they crossed the snow-covered Alps they used their shields to toboggan, hurtling down the slopes at great speed emitting the most fearful yells.

What concerns us here is their treatment of the spoils of war. After an early victory against the Romans at Orange in 105 BC the writer Orosius describes how the clothes of the Romans were shredded up and thrown away, gold and silver were thrown in the river, armour and horse-trappings were smashed while the horses themselves were drowned. He concludes, 'In short there was no more booty for the victors than pity for the vanquished.' This might sound like mere wanton destruction, but it was more than that for, as Orosius says, 'All spoils were destroyed in accordance with a new and unaccustomed vow.' By this he presumably means it was offered up to the gods in a way unfamiliar to the Romans. The description, then, makes it clear that much of the booty was thrown into a river, thus providing us with one suggestion of how some of the river finds may have originated.

Many sacrificial deposits of the utmost interest have been found in Denmark, the supposed homeland of the Cimbri: here we have the opportunity to mention only two. The first was found on the Danish island of Als, close to a farm called Hjortspring. In 1920 the local farmer was digging blocks of peat for his fire from a nearby dried-up bog, when he came upon fragments of ancient tools and weapons. These he fortunately reported to the Danish National Museum in Copenhagen, which sent an archaeologist, Dr Rosenberg, to investigate. For two years he laboured there with a team of archaeologists and by the end they had laid bare an almost complete boat, dating to the second century BC, which had been filled with the spoils of war, as well as a number of sacrificed animals, and then dragged into the middle of a swampy hollow.

The boat, over forty feet (twelve metres) long and six feet (1·83 metres) wide, was clinker-built of planks of lime wood which had been 'sewn' together with cords of bast and the joints caulked with resin. They were kept in place by ribs of hazel. It had been propelled by means of twenty paddles, while at each end strong steering oars were found, implying that it could go either backwards or forwards without having to turn round.

The offerings found inside were for the most part weapons: eight swords, 138 iron-headed spears, about twenty or so coats of iron ring-mail, and more than fifty wooden shields. In addition, the bones of a number of sacrificed animals were recovered, together with a few domestic artefacts. In view of what we now know of the habits of the Germanic peoples at this time it is tempting to see the Hjortspring deposit as an offering to the gods, possibly of spoils of war taken from the crew of a defeated raiding vessel. Perhaps it had attacked the island and had been captured by the local population.

The tradition of sacrificing boats to the gods was long-lived in Denmark. In 1858 another remarkable bog find was made, this time in Schleswig at a place called Nydam. Excavations began in 1858 and continued until 1864, when the work was interrupted by the German invasion of Denmark, after which this particular area was ceded to Germany. Excavations continued under the Germans, to the evident dissatisfaction of the original Danish excavator, who wrote somewhat scornfully of the poor quality of the work of his successors, the 'German princes and Prussian barons'. The Nydam find, dating to the fourth century AD, consisted of three or more boats, one of which was sufficiently well preserved to be removed to the Gottorp Castle Museum in Schleswig (Germany). Substantially intact, it was seventy feet (21 metres) long and clinker-built, constructed of eleven boards, one serving as the keel, with the others arranged five on each side. Along each side were fifteen rowlocks for the oars, showing that the correct complement was thirty rowers and one steersman who plied the heavy steering oar at the stern. Unlike the earlier Hjortspring boat, the Nydam vessel was fastened together with heavy iron nails.

At the time of the final ritual the boat had been loaded with offerings, a hundred swords, 500 to 600 spears and javelins, forty bows and 170 iron-tipped arrows, most of them neatly tied up in heaps and wrapped in linen. In addition, a number of objects such as Roman coins, dress fittings and ornaments, and iron tools including a fine scythe, had been loaded on board. When all was ready the boat was holed and allowed to sink.

The similarities between the two discoveries are impressive, even though at least five hundred years separate them. The Roman conquest might have engulfed the whole of Europe south of the Rhine, and Roman-made possessions might have become very acceptable in free Europe, but the rituals and the superstitions of the people were clearly little affected. The old gods and old ways prevailed.

Who the gods were who were revered at Hjortspring and Nydam we do not know for certain, but since the deposits seem to contain the spoils of war, one can guess that it was probably one or more of the fearsome Germanic gods, Odin, Thor and Tyr, who had to be placated for victory gained, and in anticipation of victories to come.

Further south, within the limits of the Roman Empire, local native deities were readily absorbed into the highly catholic assemblage of gods and demi-gods so typical of early Roman provinces. Apart from the druidic religion with its adherence to human sacrifice, which the Roman authorities detested and did their utmost to stamp out, native gods were encouraged or at least tolerated, and when one of them happened to have the same attributes as a traditional Roman deity, Roman commonsense assumed them to be one and the same, so that they would be worshipped as one, sometimes under a dual name.

One native deity who deserves consideration is Nehalennia, a goddess who looked after traders and seamen. She seems to have been a native of the region which is now Holland. The first inkling of her existence came as long ago as 1647, when a number of altars and statues were found on the island of Walcheren, near Domburg, where a sanctuary must have existed. Then, dramatically, on 14 April 1970, the goddess sprang back into the news. On that day a fisherman who was trawling in the estuary of the East Scheldt river dragged to the surface fragments of votive altars. A few months later the National Museum of Antiquities at Leiden organised a thorough investigation of the site, and soon they were able to explain what had happened. In Roman times this immediate area had been dry land, overlooking the River Scheldt: here stood a temple to the

The base of an altar to the goddess Nehalennia. The carving of a small craft loaded with wine barrels is a reminder that the goddess was the patron of merchants.

goddess significantly sited to be in full view of merchant seamen returning home after trading with the coastal areas of Britain and Gaul, or sailing forth to serve these overseas markets. It is even possible that they stopped on the way to offer a sacrifice to the goddess for their safe journey. Towards the end of the third century AD, when this area of Zeeland was gradually passing from Roman control, a series of alterations to the coastline occurred, caused by a rise in sea level. As the sea encroached, the channel deepened and its banks eroded back, until the site of the old temple was undermined and the building, together with its statues and altars, was washed into the estuary to lie undisturbed until the fishing boat came across it in 1970.

Conventional underwater excavation at a depth of eighty-five feet (twenty-six metres) was impossible. The archaeologists therefore employed a trawler and a diver, and in a period of about four weeks they brought to the surface a grand haul of 101 altars and three statues, for the most part in excellent condition. A further

One of the many votive altars to the goddess Nehalennia dredged from the bed of the River Scheldt. The goddess is seated holding a bowl of fruit with a hound at her feet.

session in 1971 yielded an additional twenty-one altars. Already the find has produced one of the largest collections of religious dedications from any temple in temperate Europe—and this is only a beginning for more work is now planned.

Nehalennia's altars ended up at the bottom of the river by the hand of nature, but some deities required that offerings should be committed to the water by the suppliant himself: such a goddess was Sequana whose sanctuary protected the source of the River Seine about twenty-two miles (35·3 kilometres) north-west of Dijon.

The delightful wooded valley where the Seine rises was provided with an extensive temple complex in the Roman period, centred on a pool and spring. The remains were well known and much dug over by the early French antiquarians, and in 1867, on nearby land owned by the city of Paris, an artificial grotto complete with nymph was created in a flourish of the antiquarian pride so characteristic of the reign of Napoleon III. Excavations continued sporadically in the early part of this century, culminating in the 1930s with the discovery of a magnificent statuette of the goddess heavily draped,

94

wearing a gown and with hands outstretched, standing in a boat modelled in the form of a swan holding a fruit in its beak. By 1953 the site had become overgrown and somewhat ramshackle. It was therefore decided to undertake a thorough study of the remains, hand-in-hand with restoration work. Several buildings were already known, including two temples, a colonnaded precinct and an enclosure identified as a ritual bathing pool. In 1963 Professor Roland Martin, who was in charge of the work, decided to drain the pool and clear it, partly to tidy up what was by then an unsightly

The goddess Sequana, from her shrine at the source of the Seine.

95

OPPOSITE
The Great Bath in the
Roman thermal baths
of Bath.

marshy area and partly in the hope of obtaining further dating evidence in an area which he knew had not been much disturbed by previous excavators. Work proceeded slowly with little result, until suddenly, on Friday 13 September, about a dozen wooden heads and wooden figurines were found preserved in the waterlogged layers. By the end of the operation no fewer than 190 had been recovered.

It soon became clear that the excavators had discovered a ritual deposit of the very greatest interest—not, as originally thought, in a bath or basin, but against a terrace wall along the edge of the sacred area. It is possible that the objects were moved there during the first century AD at a time when the old Gaulish shrine was rebuilt in masonry. An alternative explanation, that they represent the stock in trade of a craftsman selling votive objects to the pilgrims, seems less likely.

The collection is fascinating, not only for the insight it gives into the artistic ability of the wood carvers, but for the way in which it reflects the worshippers themselves and their hopes and problems. Many of the objects were heads ranging from full-size to half-size, carved with great simplicity from columns of oak heart-wood, others consisted of trunks between the neck and thighs; there were also representations of limbs, usually legs, but including a few hands. Other naturalistic carvings included animals, such as horses and a bull. Of the twenty-seven complete human statues or statuettes, most of them were depicted as wearing cloaks, either full length or knee length, some with their hoods up over the head, others with the hoods muffling the neck. The general impression given is one of great feeling for simple lines combined with a crude vigour. Yet the delicate litheness of one of the female figurines, draped in a long dress and with an arm folded across the body, is a reminder that one at least of the craftsmen possessed outstanding ability.

Perhaps most remarkable were twenty-two plaques of wood carved in relief to represent the internal organs of the human body. One of them gives a striking impression of what is thought to be a trachea and lungs enclosed within a rib-cage. Earlier discoveries included a splendid range of similar items in bronze or stone. In addition to the usual heads, hands and feet, there were models of sexual organs, breasts, and eyes, together with representations of people suffering from diseases such as goitre, hernias, arthritis, tumours and blindness.

There can be very little doubt that many of the pilgrims who

Wooden male figure wearing a short cloak from Sequana's shrine at the source of the Seine.

96

Hadrian's Wall: a symbol of the confrontation between Roman and native. For 250 years it served, when fully manned, to keep the barbarians out of Britain. Then in the late fourth century AD it was overrun by the Picts at the time of the 'Barbarian Conspiracy'.

visited Sequana's shrine suffered from illnesses and disabilities of which they hoped to be cured. One sure way of attracting the attention of the deity to a particular ailment was to present her with a model or carving as a reminder, in anticipation perhaps that the disease would be transferred to the model and thus drawn away from the body. We can imagine the pilgrims arriving at the shrine and buying from the local traders a suitable representation to present to the goddess. When this part of the devotions was over they would withdraw, possibly to the colonnades of the temple, to lie and meditate while the healing powers were being applied. The anguish as they waited must have been unbearable. How many miraculous cures the goddess could claim, how many pilgrims gradually recovered, how many continued to suffer, we will never know, but the little wooden offerings brought to light on that September day in 1963 will remain a constant and touching reminder of the simple faith of the Gaulish people.

Sequana's spring could offer no healing mineral waters to pilgrims —only hope; but there were many sources in Europe where the water itself, because of its mineral content, had well-defined medicinal properties. Such a spring, known as Les Roches, emerged from the earth at Chamalières, not far from Clermont-Ferrand in central France, close to the Gaulish citadel of Gergovia from which Caesar had been repelled with such devastating casualties during his campaigns against Vercingetorix (see Chapter 2). In 1845 a few wooden ex-votos came to light at Les Roches, together with scraps of other Roman material, but little attention was paid to the site until 1968 when modern building work was due to begin. Since the site was of potential archaeological interest, Professor Claude Vatin organised a rescue excavation; and that autumn the excavators were rewarded with a magnificent discovery—a deposit of wooden ex-votos over three feet (0·91 metres) deep and covering an area of sixty feet (eighteen metres) across—around the vents where two small springs had once emerged. In and around the deposit were found sufficient coins and pottery to show that the shrine had had a comparatively short life, following the conquest in 52–1 BC and lasting no later than the reign of Nero in the middle of the first century AD. Why the spring was abandoned so early as a cult centre is difficult to say, unless it was something to do with the growth in importance of the thermal bathing establishments at Royat and Vichy.

The wooden carvings recovered from the mud are astonishing,

Wooden carving of a human leg. Votive offering from Chamalières.

97

both in their variety and quality. In range they cover much the same subjects as those found at the source of the Seine; full figures sometimes dressed in travellers' cloaks, heads and busts, arms and legs, animals and internal organs, while the quality varies from simple, crude renderings indistinguishable from unfinished rough-outs, to refined works clearly inspired by Greek and Roman statuary. Suggestions of illness or deformity are very rare, but some hint of the spring's reputed properties is given by a head of a man with only one eye and the discovery of a bronze plaque incised with repre-sentations of two eyes: it is possible that the waters were believed to be particularly good for eye troubles. There is nothing to suggest who the presiding deity was, but one of the ex-votos of a seated woman looks like a religious representation, in which case one may suppose that the deity was a goddess.

One surprising fact to emerge from the excavation is that there appear to have been no structures associated with the springs: unlike the sanctuary of Sequana, it was simply a sacred pool in a marshy valley. A very careful examination of the way in which the objects were deposited suggested to Professor Vatin that they were water-borne: either they had been thrown into a spring, or more likely they had been set up around its margins. As the spot became less frequented the rising water dislodged them and they floated around to become entangled in a mass of vegetation. Eventually the entire area was sealed by a thick layer of alluvium which served to protect and preserve the delicate wooden objects for almost 2,000 years.

Britain, like other parts of the Roman world, could boast its fair share of sacred springs and wells, but none was so elaborately adorned as the hot springs at Bath, which gushed out of the ground at the rate of a quarter of a million gallons a day. It is not difficult to imagine the scene at the time of the Roman conquest in AD 43. Look-ing down from one of the neighbouring hills, the traveller would have had the impression of standing on the rim of a great natural basin in the bottom of which lay a level terrace, no doubt wooded, enclosed on three sides by a loop in the course of the River Avon. Towards the centre of the terrace was a large marshy swamp with two smaller patches of marsh nearby. From all three, rivulets of water drained down into the river, while over the marshes hung a pall of steam. On a cold winter's day steam would have filled the valley, leaving only the tops of the tallest trees standing gaunt above the enveloping white blanket. This dramatic scene, with its springs of hot bubbling water coating everything with a thick red crust of mineral salts, cannot have failed to impress early man. What use the pre-Roman population made of the spring we do not know, but it is inconceivable that it failed to develop as a place of pilgrimage and worship, where perhaps wooden ex-votos were offered to the presiding deity. The reason for our ignorance of these early times is that within a few decades of the invasion, the Romans began to construct a magnificent religious centre of their own around the springs.

The Roman writer Solinus, writing in the third century, gives some hint of what was there. He describes hot springs 'furnished luxuriously for human use', and goes on to say that 'over these springs Minerva presides, and in her temple the perpetual fire never whitens to ash, but as the flame fades turns into rocky lumps'—a reference, surely, to the use of local coal on the altar fires.

The luxurious buildings to which Solinus refers were short-lived. Built towards the end of the first century and repaired and modified several times, they were abandoned in the early fifth century and though still standing in part of the Saxon period, they had disappeared from sight by the beginning of the Middle Ages. As a medieval city, Bath first flourished and then declined, to rise again, in the eighteenth century, to the full glory of its Georgian elegance. The new spate of building work, which gradually gained momentum after the visit of Queen Anne, was the direct cause of the discovery of the Roman sacred area. In the summer of 1727 workmen were digging a trench for a new sewer through the middle of the main thoroughfare, Stall Street: in places it reached a depth of twenty feet (six metres) and was clearly being hacked through thick layers of Roman building debris, when in the mud there appeared a life-size gilded bronze head. Later inspection showed that it was a representation of Minerva sufficiently fine to have served as the cult statue in the temple complex. The head had been wrenched off the body, but even to this day no other part of the statue has come to light. Quite possibly it lies nearby, still twenty feet (six metres) below the street, awaiting discovery.

The unearthing of Minerva's head marked the beginning of a series of discoveries which were to continue to be made for nearly 250 years, but it was not until 1790 that the problem of Minerva's temple was raised again, this time when the old Pump Room, on Stall Street, was being rebuilt. At a depth of twelve feet (3·66 metres) below the road-level, workmen found a Roman pavement and

The temple of Sulis
Minerva and the
sacred spring at Bath.

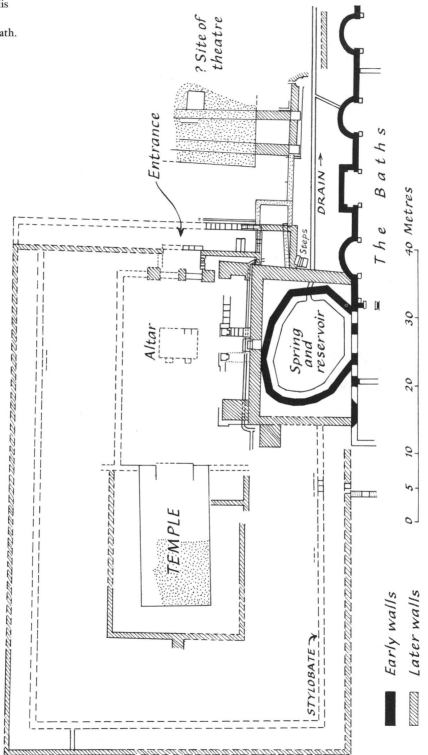

? Site of theatre

Entrance

The Baths

DRAIN →

40 Metres

Altar

Spring and reservoir

Steps

30

20

10

5

0

TEMPLE

STYLOBATE →

Early walls

Later walls

Gilded bronze head
of Minerva found in
the sewer trench in
Stall Street, Bath.

several large stone steps, but what riveted the attention of the local
antiquarians were the seventy or so large sculptured blocks that lay
tumbled in the soil above. It soon became clear that the workmen
had stumbled upon the collapsed front of the temple itself. A few
years later Samuel Lysons produced a most meticulously illustrated
account of the find and showed how the pieces fitted together to
form the pediment of a classical-style temple enclosed by an elaborate cornice and supported on four fluted columns with Corinthian
capitals. It was the pediment itself which caused the most comment.
In the centre, held aloft on a shield supported by two winged victories, was a dramatic representation of a Gorgon's head, easily identifiable by the snakes entwined in the matted hair. The face itself was
that of a pure Celt, with heavy frowning brows, a thick wedge-shaped
nose and long drooping moustaches. There can be no doubt that it
was carved by a native craftsman brought up in the Celtic tradition
but working to adorn a monument that was otherwise purely Roman
in its conception. That the pediment belonged to the temple of

Gorgon's head from the centre of the pediment of the temple of Sulis-Minerva at Bath.

Minerva was clearly demonstrated by an owl and a dolphin-crested helmet carved on the pediment below the shield: both are attributes commonly associated with Minerva.

At about this time altars were discovered in various parts of the town bearing dedications to 'Sulis-Minerva'. The idea of conflating a Roman and a native god was not at all uncommon in the Roman world. At Bath the Romans had presumably discovered a shrine to a native deity, Sulis, who presided over the healing springs, and had simply updated the dedication by attaching her nearest Roman equivalent, Minerva. The Celtic-style Gorgon's head and the survival of the name of the native deity remind us that Bath was on the fringe of the Roman world where strong undercurrents of Celtic culture were not far below the surface.

The discoveries of 1790 had gone some way towards locating the temple, but nothing was yet known of its plan and the layout of its precinct. In 1867, however, the old White Hart Inn, on the corner opposite the Pump Room, was demolished and rebuilding work began. Fortunately there lived in Bath at this time an extremely able amateur archaeologist, James Thomas Irvine, a Scotsman, born in Shetland and then working on the restoration of Bath Abbey as clerk of works to Sir Gilbert Scott. Irvine was fascinated by the problem of the temple and for two years, while the foundation work for the new building on the site of the White Hart Inn was being carried out, he kept a very close watch, recording everything he saw with great accuracy. The result was that he was able to trace a substantial part of the *podium* (platform) on which the temple was built as well as much of the colonnade which enclosed its precinct. At last the position of the temple had been established.

The next few decades in Bath saw the principal area of interest change from the temple to the huge Roman bathing establishment which was being uncovered nearby by the rather quarrelsome city engineer, Major Davis. Eventually, between 1893 and 1895, Davis returned to the problem of the temple by ripping up some of the floors of the Pump Room and exploring the structures beneath. By this time, however, he seems to have tired of the constant barrage of criticism he had come under: he not only failed to publish his results, but he didn't even plan them properly— instead, he replaced the floor on beams three to four feet (about a metre) above the Roman levels. What he had discovered, without apparently realising it, was the base of the sacrificial altar that stood in front of the temple steps, together with the main east entrance to the precinct and the approach to the sacred pool (page 100).

It was during the excavation of the baths that Davis and his site foreman, Richard Mann, who did most of the work, discovered the sacred spring and reservoir. In the hope of improving the drainage of the area they had decided to clear out a Roman drain which Irvine had discovered. Twenty feet below the level of the city, with the aid of lamps and with their pumps working full-time, the men worked their way along the Roman outfall drain dragging out tumbled blocks of masonry and removing hundreds of tons of waterladen mud. As they approached the area of the King's Bath the flow of hot mineral waters became so intense that they were forced to diverge from the strict confines of the drain and tunnel alongside a massive Roman wall, following it to its corner, at which point they appear to have surfaced mole-like in the cellar of the Pump Room. Davis now became interested and ordered the men down again. The tunnelling continued until they had defined three sides of a wall which evidently enclosed something of importance immediately below the medieval King's Bath—the basin in which the hot water

Grand opening of the
Roman baths after
the clearing work
of Major Davis.

was allowed to collect for bathing. There was little doubt in Davis's
mind that here lay the Roman springs. He could not resist the
temptation: the King's Bath was drained, its floor removed and the
mud and rubble beneath was excavated, exposing the great but-
tressed enclosure wall of the reservoir. It was into here, through
fissures in the natural clay which formed the floor of the reservoir,
that the mineral waters gushed from many thousands of feet below
the surface of the ground.

The spring and reservoir formed a central focus for the complex of
Roman buildings put up around it. To the south lay the baths, so
arranged that from the entrance hall a magnificent view could be
obtained across the spring to the altar itself, while for anyone in
Roman times standing in the precinct in front of the temple to the
north, the spring glimpsed through an ornamental façade would
have formed a major focus of interest. There was even provision for
access to the point at which the water flowed out of the reservoir
into the outfall drain.

The removal of the mud from the spring and the drain produced
an interesting array of offerings to the goddess; a gold ear-ring with
inset carbuncle, many coins, more than thirty engraved gem stones

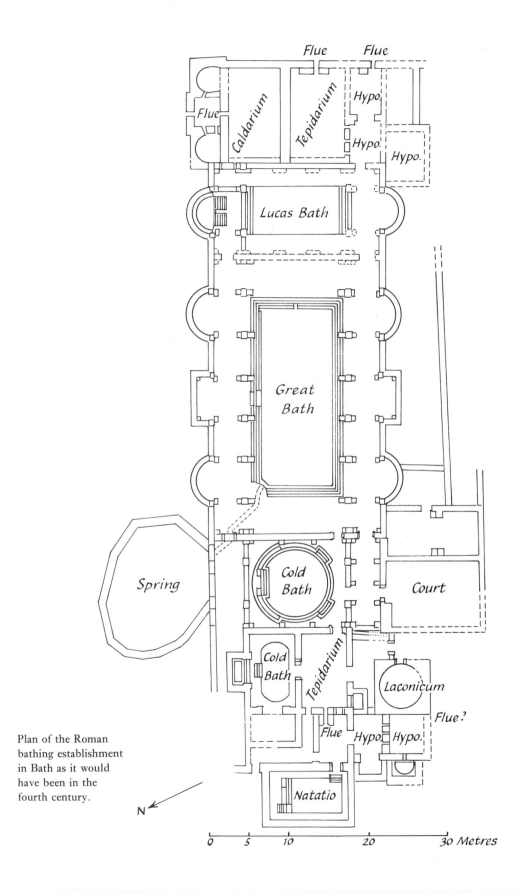

Flue   Flue

Flue

Caldarium

Tepidarium

Hypo.

Hypo.

Hypo.

Lucas Bath

Great Bath

Spring

Cold Bath

Court

Cold Bath

Tepidarium

Laconicum

Flue?

Flue

Hypo.   Hypo.

Natatio

Plan of the Roman
bathing establishment
in Bath as it would
have been in the
fourth century.

N

0   5   10   20   30 Metres

which had presumably been thrown into the water in a bag, a collection of pewter flagons and plates, a ceremonial mask of tin and a curse scratched on a small plaque of lead asking the god to damn the person who had carried off a girl called Vilbia; 'May he become as liquid as the dumb waters,' the distraught lover or parent had begged. One wonders how many wooden ex-votos had once adorned the precinct or been thrown into the reservoir. Sadly we will never know, for they would have been carried away along the drain and disgorged into the river together with so many of the offerings. We are fortunate that so much of such quality remains.

When, in 1964, a team of archaeologists led by myself came to review the evidence for the temple, it seemed to us that among the many small jobs that needed doing, such as checking the relationships and positions of walls and replanning everything in detail, the most urgent need was for the excavation of that part of the precinct which lay between the temple steps and the altar. This was easier said than done, for the entire area lay beneath the Pump Room and the Abbey yard; but eventually it was decided to cut a trench through the floor of one of the long tunnel-like cellars beneath the Pump Room. In spite of the immense difficulties—nowhere to dump the spoil, having to dig in artificial light with pumps working full-time, and the need to shore up the trench as work proceeded— the excavation was eventually completed with highly satisfactory results. Not only was the complete history of the flooding of the precinct and destruction of the temple recovered in the layers of mud and rubble through which we dug, but one major sculpture and a fine inscription were found.

The sculptured block eventually proved to be the corner of the sacrificial altar itself, one side carved with a representation of Bacchus, the other with that of a female deity. By an amazing coincidence, a second corner had been discovered nearby in 1790, while a third is now incorporated in the buttress of a church seven miles (11.2 kilometres) from Bath. The inscribed block stood in front of the altar serving as the base for a statue. It says quite simply: 'To the goddess Sulis, Lucius Marcius Memor, augurer, gave this gift'— an act of piety to the deity on the part of one of the temple officials.

The work at Bath is now temporarily at an end, but the last trench dug in the cellars beneath the Pump Room in 1968 vividly demonstrated the potential of the site. Above the temple floor was a layer of mud some five feet (1.52 metres) thick, packed solid with large limestone blocks which had tumbled from nearby monuments. All

OPPOSITE
Trial trench excavated beneath the Pump Room, Bath, 1965. The statue base with its dedication to Sulis is in its original position on the paved floor of the temple precinct.

West end of the great bathing establishment exposed in an excavation carried out in 1971. The hypocausts under two heated rooms can be seen on the left with an oval cold bath (*bottom right*). At the top left the walls of the bath built by Major Davis can be seen cutting down into the Roman levels.

were carefully worked and many showed signs of sculptured decoration. There can be little doubt that there are still major, perhaps spectacular, discoveries to be made when, eventually, we are able to return to the cellars and continue the work.

This survey of a few of the shrines in Roman Europe and beyond has necessarily been brief. From deserted bogs on Danish islands to dank cellars beneath elegant eighteenth-century buildings in Bath, the evidence of the religious life of the people continues to be found. Already there are many hundreds, even thousands, of sacred locations known; how many remain undiscovered cannot begin to be estimated, but we are left with the undeniable impression that for travellers through the Roman countryside the gods were everywhere to be found. The traders and the army introduced new gods, fashion demanded that others were adopted by the rich; their temples sprang up in the towns and in the civilian settlements outside the forts. But elsewhere, in the countryside, on isolated hilltops, in the deep woods and in the pools and springs, the old native gods lingered on.

7

Rome in Retreat

Julius Caesar's exploits marked the beginning of overt imperialism—great tracts of Europe fell under Roman domination. Under Augustus there was further expansion and consolidation and even in the early years of the second century AD Trajan was forcing the frontiers back deep into barbarian Europe. But this was to be virtually the end of Rome's aggressive policies—the limits of internal stability had been reached, and in some places exceeded. Trajan's successor, Hadrian (117–138), saw himself as the consolidator, the frontier builder, intent on creating a stable world in which art and culture could develop. His immediate successors, though forced to campaign against the northern barbarians, did so largely to maintain internal stability. Thus by the second half of the second century, an acceptable equilibrium had been reached—Rome seemed destined to last a millennium.

The crisis came in the third century. In the 220s the powerful Sassanids from Persia attacked Mesopotamia, Armenia and Syria; in the 230s the German Alamanni began a series of assaults on the Rhine and Danube provinces, while the Goths moved against the lower Danube; a few years later the provinces of Africa and Egypt began to come under barbarian attack. The first province to crumble was Dacia, when, following intolerable pressures from the tribes to the north and east, Aurelian finally withdrew to the south of the Danube in 271. It was an admission of defeat: henceforth the Rhine and Danube were to form the boundary to the Roman world —at least for a while.

From the late third century onwards, the frontiers became increasingly strongly defended. Towns were given defensive walls, fortified road stations were built for the protection of travellers, villas were sometimes defended, new forts were built and a rash of look-out posts and watch towers sprang up to provide early warning of enemy troop movements. Different communities responded in different ways, but the result was always the same—a retreat behind defences.

In the earlier chapters we have tended to emphasise the 'them and us' attitude to the Roman Empire—a frontier, with Romans on one side and barbarians on the other. While the reality of the frontier line cannot be disputed for the early centuries of the Empire, and the presence of the barbarian hordes always ready to break through was an ever-present and grim reality, the situation in the late third and throughout the fourth century was rather more complex. In the north-western part of the mainland European Empire south of the Rhine, that is the provinces of Lower Germany and Gallia Belgica, it is possible to begin to piece together something of this fascinating picture.

The people living to the north of the frontier, in northern Holland and Germany, were, from the end of the second century onwards, subject to three pressures: the population was growing rapidly, change in the sea level was causing the inundation of vast areas of once fertile coastland, and the Germanic tribes to the east, themselves under pressure from farther east, were pressing in. The only escape lay south across the frontier.

To the south the Roman provinces were suffering from rather different social and economic ills. There appears to have been serious depopulation in the countryside, caused partly by a decrease in the birth rate, and partly by a general atmosphere of discontent which led some people to migrate to the towns while others broke away and joined gangs of bandits (*bagaudae*) who were roaming the country-side. For the Roman administration the situation was very serious. A thinly populated countryside made defence difficult and this area was particularly crucial because it was where the Rhine frontier-command met the coastal command, later to be put under the control of an officer entitled the Count of the Saxon Shore: well-defended lines of communication to enable troops to be moved at a moment's notice were absolutely vital.

Faced with these dual problems, pressure from the barbarians outside and depopulation within, the administration took the logical course. From the second half of the third century into the early part of the fourth, bands of barbarians were brought south to settle

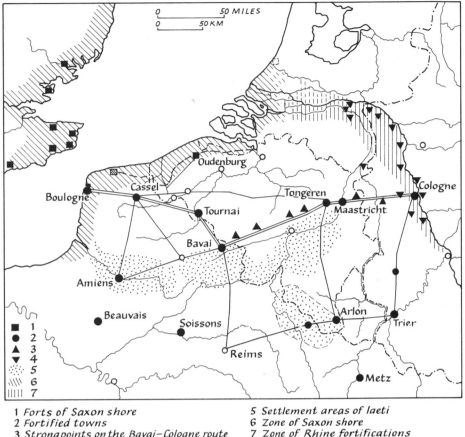

1 *Forts of Saxon shore*
2 *Fortified towns*
3 *Strongpoints on the Bavai–Cologne route*
4 *Rhine fortifications*

5 *Settlement areas of laeti*
6 *Zone of Saxon shore*
7 *Zone of Rhine fortifications*

The north-western part of the Roman frontier zone in the fourth century AD.

in the depopulated lands, in a broad sweep from the region of Amiens across to Trier. These communities were called *laeti*, a generalised term which included a number of different tribal groups such as Frisians and Franks. The exact status of these settlers is difficult to untangle. One text gives the impression that they were distributed between the large landowners to serve as serfs on the estates, but it is clear that other groups were organised into quasi-military units under the overall charge of *praefecti*. There was probably considerable variation from place to place, but the overall policy seems to have been that the *laeti* were given land to farm and were expected to be in a state of military readiness to protect the territory against further barbarian pressures from north of the Rhine.

Some years ago it was thought that the Rhine frontier north of Cologne was abandoned after the raids of the 260s, and a new line of defence created along the road that leads due west from Cologne to Boulogne on the north French coast, immediately south of which the *laeti* were settled. The kind of evidence quoted was that all the towns along the line—Cassel, Tournai, Bavai, Tongeren and Maastricht—were heavily defended, while at regular intervals along the road, defended road-stations were built at places like Liberchies, Taviers and Braives, where squarish earthworks have been found pre-dating *c*. 275. More recently it has been shown that many more of the forts along the lower Rhine were defended in a later period than was previously believed, while an unexpected fort has been discovered on the coast at Oudenburg between Boulogne and the mouth of the Rhine. Clearly the old frontiers, the Rhine and the coast, remained in use to the end. What then of the Cologne-Boulogne line? One reason for its exceptionally strong defences must have been its importance as a line of communication between the Rhine command and the coastal defences: messages had to be passed and troops moved with speed and safety; overnight refuges were essential. But could not another reason be the presence of the *laeti* themselves? It would have been dangerous to have allowed them free access to the rear of the frontier line; barbarians on both sides of the river would have posed an intolerable hazard. It is tempting, therefore, to think that one of the functions of the Cologne-Boulogne line was to prevent the *laeti* from penetrating too far north towards the military zone: at this stage even allies were potential enemies.

The fort at Oudenburg on the Belgian coast deserves a brief discussion, for its discovery has thrown new light on the coastal defences in the late third and fourth centuries. One text which survives, a late Roman army list called the *Notitia Dignitatum*, mentions that some of the maritime regions of Gaul were under a commander called the *Dux Belgicae Secundae* and that there were units stationed at three separate locations, none of which could with certainty be identified. Belgian archaeologists looking for the sites are under considerable difficulties because the coastline has changed so much since the fourth century; but from a careful study of the silting patterns they have been able to establish the approximate position of the high-water mark. One site in particular, the village of Oudenburg, attracted the attention of Dr J. Mertens when he began to study the problem. In the Middle Ages Oudenburg was an important maritime town which was graced with an abbey—the abbey of St Peter. Now, in a chronicle written between 1084 and 1087 we learn how the monks obtained building-stone for the

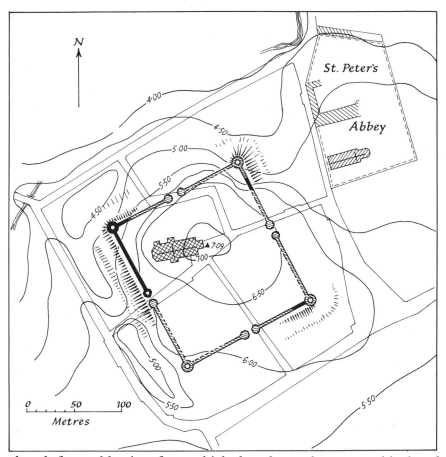

The late Roman fortress at Oudenburg. The plan has been reconstructed on the basis of traces of walls found in excavations, shown here in black. The shape of the fort has determined the present-day street plan.

church from old ruins, from which they dragged out great blocks of stone derived from Tournai, Boulogne and the Rhine area. At the same time we read that they discovered pottery and various beautiful objects. The evidence was clearly and very strongly suggestive of a large Roman structure, but it did not, of course, give its location. Dr Mertens therefore had to turn to the present street plan: he observed that the streets and building plots were arranged suggestively within a square and that this layout had been determined by a twelfth-century defensive ditch. From this evidence it was almost certain that the medieval ditch had originally followed the line of the Roman wall. Trial trenches were cut across the supposed line in 1956 and '57 and confirmed its existence beyond any doubt. The wall itself no longer survived, only the trench where it had once been built; for just as the abbey chronicle had said, all the stone had been robbed, but within the debris left behind, fragments of the three types of stone mentioned were found.

What was discovered at Oudenburg was a fort some 500 feet (152 metres) by 450 feet (137 metres), protected by a V-shaped ditch, with a gate in the centre of each side flanked by massive bastions, and with bastions at each corner. From the evidence of the coins and pottery it would seem that the masonry fort was constructed in the early part of the fourth century, but before that the site had been occupied by another earth-and-timber fort which may well have belonged to the period of the troubles in the 260s or perhaps a little later. The situation, right on the edge of the sea, leaves little doubt that the forts were occupied by garrisons of marine commandos, able to drive off an enemy who was attacking by land or take to the ships and engage pirate raiders on the open sea.

The discovery of the Roman fort at Oudenburg is a fine example of archaeological detective work. Starting with a general hypothesis based on one kind of evidence, the Belgian archaeologists worked through different kinds of data until with one neatly-defined series of excavations they were able to convert reasonable theory into positive fact.

The location of the other two sites mentioned by the *Notitia* as being under the command of the *Dux Belgicae Secundae* still remains uncertain. One is referred to by the name of *Marcis*, which could be Marck near Calais or Marquise near Boulogne, but this is pure guesswork. The other is described as the base of the *Classis Sambrica* (Sambrican fleet). Here we are on slightly firmer ground, for in 1873 at Étaples, south of Boulogne, some Roman tiles were found stamped with the letters CLSAM and CLSAMA, which are quite reasonably interpreted as an abbreviation of *Classis Sambrica*. But until careful fieldwork and planned excavation of the kind carried out at Oudenburg is undertaken along the north French coast, the exact whereabouts of these two important sites will remain unknown.

For Britain the problem of coastal protection was particularly serious. The island was beset by enemies on all sides. From north of Hadrian's Wall came the Picts, from Ireland the Scots and the Irish, from the Western Isles, the Attacotti, while across the North Sea lay the lands of the Saxons and Franks. Britain was above all vulnerable to attack from the sea—its frontiers were its coasts, and the North Sea was a breeding ground for barbarian pirates. The situation had become so serious by the mid 280s that Rome was forced to take special steps to cope with the pirates by appointing a Belgian named Carausius to 'rid the seas of Belgica and Armorica of pirates', that is the North Sea and the English Channel. Carausius

Portchester Castle, Hampshire, one of the forts built by Carausius against pirate attacks in the late third century AD. The outer walls with their forward-projecting bastions are Roman. The church and castle are Norman.

seems to have met with a degree of success, but was eventually forced for political reasons to set himself up as Emperor of Britain to escape retribution from his enemies in Rome. He had in fact been accused of being in league with the pirates and sharing their booty with them! The story ended with his murder followed by the eventual restoration of central government in 296.

The pirate menace hovered in the background throughout the early decades of the fourth century, but in 360 the barbarian raids began once more in earnest. In that year the Scots from northern Ireland and the Picts from central Scotland swept down on the frontier regions, and it was not until a special force of four detachments of *comitatenses* (field army) was sent under the general Lupicinus that the situation in Britain was brought under control. Five years later the Picts, Scots and Attacotti attacked again, and in 367 the full force of the barbarian assault broke. This was the year of the 'Barbarian Conspiracy'. Picts, Scots and Attacotti descended on the province from the north, while the Saxons and Franks were active in the North Sea, raiding the coasts of Gaul and possibly Britain. The word 'conspiracy' used by a Roman commentator implies that the attack was co-ordinated. At any event it was a notable success. Hadrian's Wall, though fully garrisoned, was overrun, the officer in charge of the shore defences was killed, and the military commander in Britain taken prisoner. In the confusion which followed, soldiers deserted and slaves ran away to join the parties of raiders who roamed the country. Britain, we are told, was in a state of chaos as far south as the Thames.

Once more the central government was forced to intervene with military support. Eventually Count Theodosius was put in charge, and with four regiments of the field army he landed at Richborough in Kent and proceeded to London. From here he began a far-sighted programme of restoration, first offering amnesty to the deserters and then systematically clearing the province of barbarians and dissidents. As this work proceeded he set about repairing defences and reorganising garrisons. It was probably at this time that many of the walled towns of Britain were provided with forward-projecting bastions, upon which they could mount artillery such as catapults and stone-throwing machinery to fight off attack. The emphasis was now firmly upon defence.

One of the lessons learned from the 'Barbarian Conspiracy' was that Hadrian's Wall, however strongly manned, could easily be outflanked by a maritime enemy. All the Picts had to do was to sail around the end of the frontier zone and land on the Yorkshire coast. It was no doubt as a response to this potential threat that Theodosius devised a completely new defensive scheme—a series of watch towers high up on the cliffs, so sited that they could observe enemy movements at sea and signal to the Roman fleet to form up ready for the attack. Five signal stations are now known—Huntcliff, Goldsborough, Ravenscar, Scarborough and Filey—all brilliantly sited to have extensive views of the North Sea, and to be inter-visible one with another. A network of roads would have linked them to the military base at Malton and ultimately to the legionary fortress at York, between thirty-five and forty-five miles (56·3 and 72·4 kilometres) inland.

Castle Hill,
Scarborough, the site
of one of the signal sta-
tions which guarded the
Yorkshire coast in the
late fourth century AD.

A general awareness that these sites existed can be traced back to 1774, when during the construction of Ravenscar Hall an inscription was found. It was quite small, only twenty-two by fifteen inches (0·56 by 0·40 metres), with letters crudely cut with a pick. It records simply that 'Justinianus, commander; Vindicianus, *magister*, built this tower and fort from ground level' (*magister* was a low rank in the late Roman army). Tower and fort, as we shall see, is an extremely accurate description of a typical Yorkshire signal station. About the middle of the last century the station at Huntcliff was discovered, and eventually excavated in 1911–12; Filey was first noted in 1857, and excavated in 1923; Scarborough in 1919.

The discovery of Goldsborough in 1918 was the result of organised field work by two local archaeologists, William Hornsby and John Laverick. Following the excavation of Huntcliff they guessed that another signal station should exist somewhere between it and Ravenscar. After abortive searching at Rockcliff-by-Boulby, a headland 660 feet (201 metres) high, they came to Goldsborough Pasture with its magnificent views of the sea described by the excavators: 'To the left lies Runswick, with its glorious bay. To the right is Whitby, with the Abbey and harbour, while behind stretches the moorland, black and lonesome, still reputed the abode of evil spirits.' Within half an hour of locating the site they had dug a trial hole in which undisputed late Roman pottery turned up. The excavation which followed revealed a signal station in a fine state of preservation—together with gruesome evidence of the dangers of life at the end of the Roman era.

The defensive wall at Goldsborough enclosed an area just over a hundred feet (30·5 metres) across: it was four feet (1·22 metres) thick, and at each corner was thickened so as to form completely circular bastions to serve as platforms for mounted artillery such as *ballistas* capable of firing volleys of arrows at would-be attackers. To keep the assailants in range, a V-shaped ditch had been dug around the wall, but at a distance of over thirty feet (nine metres) from it. Anyone approaching the fortlet would be hindered by the obstacle for a sufficient length of time for the artillery to be brought into effective action. Only one entrance was provided through the fort wall and here the wall was inturned to form a passageway which was probably surmounted by a tower or at least a fighting platform, access to which was by means of a flight of steps.

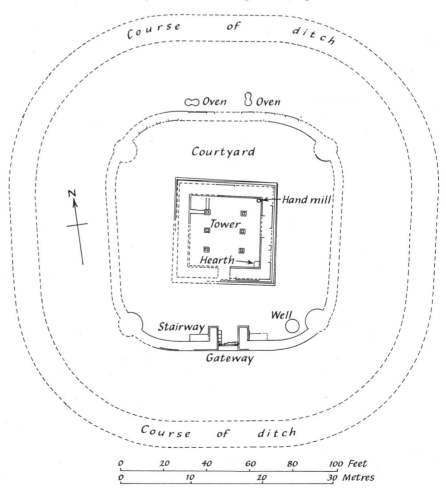

The late Roman signal station at Goldsborough, Yorkshire.

Once inside the gate, the intruder would have been confronted by the great watch tower, nearly fifty feet (15 metres) square and with walls five feet (1·52 metres) thick at the base. Such massive foundations would probably have supported a superstructure up to a hundred feet (thirty metres) high. A single door led into the ground floor of the tower, where six stone bases were discovered, presumably once supporting timbers taking the weight of the upper floors. Judging from the amount of pottery and animal bones and from the well discovered in the corner of the walled enclosure, the guards must have lived on the spot, probably using the tower for shelter. Two ovens found outside the wall between it and the ditch suggest that at times the space within the wall was not sufficient and cooking was done outside in the open.

The signal station must have been a fairly austere place to live, windy, lonely and dangerous. It was just inside the tower that the excavators came upon grim evidence of the last horrors. The description deserves to be given in their own words:

'In the south-east corner, we made discoveries which can only be described as sensational. A short, thick-set man had fallen across the smouldering fire of an open hearth, probably after having been stabbed in the back. His skeleton lay face downwards, the left hand, on which was a bronze ring, behind the back, the right touching the south wall. Another skeleton, that of a taller man, lay also face downwards, near the feet of the first, his head pointing south-west. Beneath him was the skeleton of a large, powerful dog, its head against the man's throat, its paws across his shoulders—surely a grim record of a thrilling drama, perhaps the dog one of the defenders, the man an intruder.'

When the human bones were later studied by Sir Arthur Keith at the Royal College of Surgeons, he was able to add further details about the man lying across the hearth. At or very soon after the moment of death 'he received across the top of the head a series of blows with the cutting edge of a weapon such as a sword, several being ineffective but one which cleft through the whole thickness of the vault. A twist of the swordsman's wrist has wrenched out a considerable fragment from the upper occipital part of the skull behind the line of cleavage. The skull has also been crushed in by a heavy blow ... (which) also was given at or just after death, for the texture of the fractured surface is that seen only when a fresh skull is broken. There are also three punctured wounds on the left side of the skull produced by pointed weapons such as the point of a sword or a spear.' At the end of this detailed assessment Sir Arthur adds, 'that the short sturdy man died a violent death there can be no reasonable doubt.' This was not quite all; part of another skull was found on the floor of the tower, while from the well were recovered fragments of three other skulls, one of a very old man, a second of a man about fifty and the third of a young woman of about thirty.

Exactly how one interprets these details is open, at least a little, to imagination, but the grisly end of the last inhabitants of the signal station is clear enough, even though we will never know by whose hand they died.

The Rhine frontier was no safer place to be, for just across the river were the great and growing confederacies of barbarian tribes, the Franks, the Saxons, and the Alamanni, gradually increasing in number and in strength and pressing down, gently at first, on the thin line of the Roman frontier. In 215 and again in 234 the line broke, but on both occasions the situation was restored. Far more serious were the events following the fateful year 253, when the frontier troops left their posts to take sides in a civil war. The Alamanni poured across the upper Rhine into the province of Upper Germania, some of them reaching as far south as Gaul, while the Franks pillaged the territories south of the lower Rhine. Although the barbarians were eventually pushed back, it had been a devastating blow to Roman morale. In 275–6 another wave of plunderings took place, even more widespread and damaging than the previous one. This time the Emperor Probus came to the rescue and once more the battle was taken back into enemy territory, but it was clear by now that the German menace was there to stay.

During the first half of the fourth century the situation remained fairly quiet, but in 350–1 the Alamanni again took advantage of a civil war and swept down into Gaul, reaching as far south as Autun and Troyes. The Roman troops under the command of a young man, Julian, a relation of the Emperor, gradually cleared the province of Germans and in a great battle fought at Strasbourg in 357 soundly defeated the assembled barbarian forces. The victory was carefully followed up by campaigns in Germany and a systematic strengthening of the Rhine frontier. Further troubles followed in 365, which required much of the attention of the Emperor Valentinian until his death in 375, but now a new terror appeared from the east beyond the Black Sea—the Huns, and with the Huns an entirely different problem.

Until this time the Germanic raids had been little more than foraging parties engaged in collecting loot, but now under unbearable pressure from the Huns in the east the Germans were forced to look for new lands to settle, and the only possible territories lay south of the Rhine. The Emperor Valens tried to hold back further onslaughts, but was killed in 378. This marked a turning point. From now on barbarians were allowed into the crumbling Empire to settle, obeying Roman laws, yet serving under their own leaders as a military force of confederates (*foederati*) whose task was to protect frontier zones from further inroads. Gradually the policy collapsed and as civil war sapped the energies of the Western Empire, more and more barbarians crossed the frontiers to raid and to settle. Imperceptibly the northern provinces slipped back into a state of near anarchy and barbarism.

The broad historical outline offered here is sufficient to emphasise that the Rhine and Danube frontiers were extremely dangerous places in which to live or be stationed during the fourth century. Nevertheless, in the intervals between being called away to support one Imperial contender or another, a large number of men and their families were resident along the frontier zone.

One such group occupied a little fortlet called the Bürgle, on the crest of a hill overlooking the flood plain of the river Danube south of the Bavarian town of Lauingen. It was sited to keep watch over an important crossroads and to keep an eye on enemy movements across the river. The first indication that a site existed here at all came as the result of the commercial extension of a sand pit which quarried into one corner of what was soon recognised to be a Roman building. Excavation began immediately under the sponsorship of the Römisch-Germanische Kommission, and was directed by Gerhard Bersu. (Bersu left Germany soon after the Nazis came to power and took up residence in Britain, where he was to carry out a number of highly distinguished excavations of which the most famous was the large-scale stripping of the Iron Age farmstead at Little Woodbury, near Salisbury). In his absence his work was suppressed by the Nazi regime and it was not until he returned to Germany after the war that he was able to produce and publish the report on what proved to be a curious and unique structure.

The Bürgle was built on an oval hillock and protected by a ditch. Strictly it was nothing more than a pair of barrack blocks enclosed within a strong masonry wall ten feet (three metres) thick, about 200 feet (61 metres) long and 75 feet (23 metres) wide. The main gate at the east end was protected by flanking walls creating a court-yard so as to bottle up any would-be attackers. Another, smaller, gate existed at the west end, dominated by a tower. Between the two gates ran a single narrow street flanked on either side by timber-built barrack rooms built up against the fort walls, while in the south-west corner was a suite of fine rooms, one of which had underfloor heating. Each of the barrack rooms was provided with a hearth. There can be very little doubt that the accommodation was designed to house a century (a unit of eighty to a hundred men) with its junior officers.

Life was without much luxury; a range of coarse pottery, a few brooches, some bronze uniform attachments, and a glass gaming counter were all that was found, together with the iron heads of spears and *ballista* arrows. It cannot have been particularly enjoyable living in such an isolated position in such cramped and claustrophobic conditions, always having to be on guard against attack.

Bersu thought that the Bürgle could be identified with a place called Pinianis, which is mentioned in the late Roman army list known as the *Notitia Dignitatum*. The *Notitia* tells us that Pinianis was garrisoned by the First Valerian Cohort of Phrygians and its tribune, a unit raised in Asia Minor by the Emperor Valerian in the middle of the third century. There are, however, problems in this interpretation. The full cohort would at this time be between 300 and 500 men, whereas the Bürgle could house no more than a third or quarter of this number. Bersu overcame this problem by suggesting that the Bürgle was simply the fortified headquarters of the tribune and his guard, the rest of the unit being spread out in other forts. But even more serious is the fact that the accommodation was not suitable for a man of the rank of tribune. With so many doubts it is best to admit that the identity of the unit cannot with certainty be determined.

To date the period of occupation of the fortlet we must rely entirely on the evidence of the hundred coins found during the excavation. Of these, seventy-seven date to after the period 335–40, strongly suggesting that occupation did not begin until this time, the earlier coins being explained as small change already in circulation. The coin series ends with eight newly minted issues from Aquileia produced between 378 and 383. These presumably came from the soldiers' last pay packet and were lost immediately before the abandonment of the site. The year 383 would fit very well because it was in this year that Maximus, who had been serving in Britain, set himself up as Emperor, and took a large army to the Continent to support his claim, not only depleting Britain of troops, but causing frontier forces to be withdrawn to oppose him. Whether the garrison at Bürgle was ordered to the attack or whether it was left to hold the frontier, we will never know—all that is certain is that in the summer of 383 the Germans flooded south across the Rhine once more: after this the little frontier post was never brought back into use again.

Gerhard Bersu's skills as an excavator are demonstrated again in the final site to be considered, the lonely hill top of the Wittnauer Horn in the Jura mountains of Switzerland. Here on a narrow spur nearly a thousand feet (305 metres) above a marshy valley, he was able to demonstrate a series of fortifications spanning the period from the eighth century BC to the fourth century AD. The first, prehistoric, defenders turned the spur into an impregnable fortress by constructing a massive bank and ditch across the neck of the ridge. It was a colossal undertaking; even now in its decayed and eroded state the bank is still 120 feet (36·6 metres) wide and 30 feet (9 metres) high. Inside Bersu found evidence of regularly laid-out houses of permanent character, showing that people had lived here for at least part of the year. Eventually the site was abandoned and lay derelict for many centuries.

It was not until the end of the Roman era that the site was redefended once more, this time with a masonry-built wall inserted into the old grass-grown rampart. There is nothing to suggest that the work was official or part of a military defensive scheme. More likely it was the response of the rural population to the dangers and difficulties which now beset them as the civilised order of the Empire began to crumble. The wheel had gone full circle and people were reverting once more to their traditional methods of self-protection.

EPILOGUE

The end of the Empire came fast. In the space of a lifetime, from about 370–420, the civilised existence that so many knew virtually came to an end. The events of this period are tightly interwoven: Huns, Goths, Alans, Vandals, Germans—all contributed to the turmoil, creating pressures with which the decaying Roman state, racked with its own internal problems, was unable to cope.

The Goths, who had appeared from the north in the third century and had managed to conquer large tracts of South Russia, were the first major group to be forced into Europe by pressure from their eastern neighbours, the Huns. Pressure was so great that at the end of the fourth century the Roman authorities allowed the hordes to settle south of the Danube, but one of the tribes, the Visigoths, was restless and in 378 moved south through Macedonia into Greece. Twenty years later they were on the move again, this time along the Adriatic coast, and between 408 and 412 they had reached Italy and were terrorising Rome itself. Another move, encouraged by the Emperor Honorius, took them through southern France, down into Spain and finally to Aquitania in western France, where in 418 they at last decided to settle down.

Theirs was not the only migration. In the winter of 406 a vast horde of Vandals, Alans and Lugi crossed the frozen Rhine and ravaged Gaul, eventually arriving in Spain three years later. Another tribe, the Burgundians, crossed the Rhine at about the same time, and settled in the area of Alsace. Pressures on Britain also caused dislocation of population, for in 440–41 a number of Britons from Cornwall moved into Brittany.

The picture is one of roving bands of men, women and children forced out of their homelands, spreading south and west into the crumbling Roman Empire, seeking new lands. Sometimes they were in conflict with the remanent Roman armies, sometimes they worked with them to oppose further incursions.

One of the causes of the disruptions was the appearance in Europe of the Huns—originally a nomadic tribe whose home lay in the Altai Mountains of Russia. They are first mentioned in about AD 150, but thereafter occur more frequently in the historical record until in the years following 370 we hear of them destroying Gothic power in South Russia. A little later, in confederacy with the Alans and Sarmatians, they crossed the Danube into Pannonia (later to become known as Hungary) and from there terrorised neigh-

bouring parts of Europe. They were excellent horsemen: armed with·
short powerful bows, which they used from horseback with great
skill, the Hunnish armies fast gained a reputation for invincibility.
Unified under the leadership of Attila, the empire of the Huns spread
across central Europe. In 451 they were raiding deep into Gaul and
two years later were ravaging northern Italy. But in 454, after
dynastic quarrels had weakened them following Attila's death, they
were soundly beaten by the Germans. By 470 the Huns had retreated
back into Russia and were heard of no more.

With external enemies like these, how could the old Roman
Empire be expected to survive? With economic decline, a decreasing
population, plague and the breakdown of organised government,
the situation fast became impossible. Gradually the western part of
the Empire took on a new appearance as the old order became
submerged beneath the tide of newcomers. In the patchwork of
new states which now began to emerge, the familiar outlines of
modern Europe can at last dimly be recognised.

BOOKS FOR FURTHER READING

BROGAN, O., Roman Gaul (Bell, London 1953)

CAESAR, The Conquest of Gaul, *translated by F. A. Handford* (Penguin Books, Harmondsworth 1951)

FRERE, S. S., Britannia (Routledge, London 1967)

MCDONALD, A. H., Republican Rome (Thames & Hudson, London 1966)

ROSSI, L., Trajan's Column and the Dacian Wars (Thames & Hudson, London 1971)

ROSTOVTZEFF, M., Rome (Galaxy, New York 3rd edition 1963)

TACITUS, The Agricola and Germania, *translated by H. Mattingley* (Penguin Books, Harmondsworth 1970)

THOMPSON, E. A., The Early Germans (Oxford University Press, London 1965)

WEBSTER, G., The Roman Imperial Army (A. & C. Black, London 1969)

INDEX